FIRST CERTIFICATE HANDBOOK

For Cambridge First Certificate Papers 1, 2 and 3
Third Edition

Revise page 77→107   P77
Reading 161+162
Tests page 166 - 3+4.
Writing page 118
96.97. 98.

P85
P97 43.44.
     45.

P152
P104. P107.

Other EFL titles published by Stanley Thornes and Hulton:

H Naylor and C S L Hagger, *First Certificate Handbook Key*, 3rd Edition

S Greenall, *Language Games and Activities*

M J E Kassem, *Tests in English for Overseas Students*

L F Leveson with M Cass, *Skytalk: English for Air Communication*

J H Montagu Butler, *Interactive Projects*

M J Murphy, *Understanding Phrasal Verbs*

G Ramsey, *Listen In*

G Ramsey, *Let's Get Talking*

G Ramsey, *Let's Keep Talking*

G Ramsey and M Rutman, *Scenes and Themes*

P Sauvain and M Carrier, *Topics for Discussion and Language Practice*

D Sellen, *Skills in Action*

H A Swan, *New English Proficiency Course*

H A Swan, *Act One in English*

FIRST CERTIFICATE HANDBOOK

FOR CAMBRIDGE FIRST CERTIFICATE PAPERS 1, 2 AND 3

Third Edition

Helen Naylor & Stuart Hagger

Stanley Thornes (Publishers) Ltd

Text © H. Naylor and C. S. L. Hagger 1979, 1984, 1988
Illustrations © Stanley Thornes (Publishers) Ltd 1988

All rights reserved. No part of this publication may be reproduced or transmitted in any form or by any means, electronic or mechanical, including photocopy, recording, or any information storage and retrieval system, without permission in writing from the publisher or under licence from the Copyright Licensing Agency Limited. Further details of such licences (for reprographic reproduction) may be obtained from the Copyright Licensing Agency Limited, of 33–4 Alfred Place, London WC1E 7DP.

First published in Great Britain 1979
by Hulton Educational Publications Ltd

This edition published in Great Britain by
Stanley Thornes (Publishers) Ltd
Old Station Drive, Leckhampton
Cheltenham GL53 0DN UK

Reprinted 1980, 1981, 1982, 1983
Second edition 1984
Revised and reprinted 1984
Reprinted 1985
Third edition 1988
Reprinted 1989, 1990

British Library Cataloguing in Publication Data
Naylor, Helen
    First certificate handbook.—3rd ed.
    1. English language For non-English
speaking students
    I. Title   II. Hagger, Stuart
428.2′4

ISBN 0–85950–8234

This is a net book and should not be sold at a price lower than the publisher's current listed price.

Phototypeset by Tech-Set, Gateshead, Tyne & Wear
Printed in Great Britain at The Bath Press, Avon

Contents

Acknowledgements vi
General introduction vii

Paper 1 Reading Comprehension 1

Section A: Introduction 2

1 Word and preposition combinations 3
2 Phrasal verbs 4
3 General vocabulary 5
4 Idioms and other common word groups 7
5 Words which cause special difficulties 8
6 Practice and further study 9

Section B: Introduction 11

1 Finding the meaning of unknown words 12
2 Reading with clear comprehension 20
3 Dealing with multiple-choice questions on written texts 23

Paper 2 Composition 35

Introduction 36

1 Telling a story 37
2 Descriptions of people 44
3 Descriptions of places 49
4 Giving directions 52
5 Descriptions of objects 53
6 Prescribed texts 55
7 Letters to a friend 59
8 Semi-formal letters 63
9 Discursive writing 66
10 A talk or speech 70
11 Final notes on composition titles 72

Paper 3 Use of English 75

Introduction 76

1 Filling in the blanks in a passage 77
2 Sentence transformation 81
3 Changing the form of words in context 108
4 Guided sentence writing 110
5 Incomplete dialogues 111
6 Indirect and direct speech 112
7 Vocabulary and phrasal verb questions 114
8 Questions based on dialogues or texts 116
9 Questions based on other source material 120

Appendices 127

Appendix 1 Word + preposition combinations 128
Appendix 2 Preposition + word phrases 130
Appendix 3 Word building 131

Test Papers 141

Set 1 142
Set 2 151
Set 3 160

Acknowledgements

The authors wish particularly to thank Mrs H. A. Swan, the staff and students of the Swan School of English, Oxford, for all their encouragement and help.

Thanks are due to the following for allowing the use of extracts from the copyright material mentioned below:

Pergamon Press Ltd: *The Only Child*, by James Kirkup (Pergamon English Library) • Reprinted by permission of Faber and Faber Ltd: *Lord of the Flies*, by William Golding • Rosica Colin Ltd: *A Start in Life*, by Alan Sillitoe, published by W. H. Allen • John Farquharson Ltd: *Waiting* and *Twenty Pieces of Silver* by Stan Barstow • David Higham Associates Ltd: *The Unpleasantness at the Bellona Club*, by Dorothy L. Sayers, published by Victor Gollancz Ltd • Murray Pollinger: *Parson's Pleasure*, from *Kiss, Kiss*, by Roald Dahl, published by Michael Joseph Ltd and Penguin Books Ltd • Peter Davis Ltd: *Below Stairs*, by Margaret Powell • Michael Joseph Ltd: *Fresh from the Country*, by 'Miss Read' • Reprinted by permission of A. D. Peters & Co. Ltd: *The Sun King*, by Nancy Mitford, published by Hamish Hamilton Ltd • Granada Publishing Ltd: *The Whispering Land*, by Gerald Durrell, published by Rupert Hart-Davis Ltd • John Farquharson Ltd: *Annapurna South Face*, by Chris Bonington, published by Cassell & Co. Ltd • Curtis Brown Ltd: *Through the Tunnel*, from *The Habit of Loving*, by Doris Lessing, published by Granada Publishing Ltd • Reprinted by permission of Chatto & Windus Ltd: *The Sandcastle*, by Iris Murdoch • Michael Joseph Ltd: *The Desperadoes*, by Stan Barstow • John Murray Ltd: *Life Below Stairs*, by Frank E. Huggett.

The extract from the University of Cambridge Regulations for the First Certificate in English is used by kind permission of the University of Cambridge Local Examinations Syndicate.

The authors and publisher would like to thank the following for permission to reproduce copyright material: British Gas; The Post Office; Walkers Crisps Ltd; The Home Office. The Customs notice on page 155 is reproduced with the permission of the Controller of Her Majesty's Stationery Office.

We are also grateful to Mary Evans Picture Library for permission to reproduce the photograph of Albert Schweitzer on page 79 and the engraving of Louis XIV on page 118. The photographs, with the exception of page 48, are by Alan Spence of Harwell, Oxon.

General introduction

First Certificate Handbook is for students preparing for the three written papers of the Cambridge First Certificate Examination, and is intended for individuals or groups working with or without a teacher. It is based on the principle that students must be taught before they can be tested, and that attempting examination practice questions without guidance is not, in itself, adequate preparation for the First Certificate Examination.

The aims of *First Certificate Handbook* are:
- to teach the reading and writing skills needed for the examination, and
- to make students familiar with the disciplines and techniques they must master if they are to achieve their full potential in the examination.

The book can be used to fit into any course of study, whether full-time or part-time. For part-time classes preparing for the First Certificate Examination the material is sufficient for, say, two weekly lessons of one-and-a-half or two hours over a period of up to six months. For full-time classes the course thoroughly prepares students for the examination.

The vocabulary level of *First Certificate Handbook* is set, where appropriate, at Level 5 of the Cambridge English Lexicon, as specified in the Cambridge Regulations. A good English–English dictionary and a modern English grammar will be useful supplements to the course; they will be particularly important for the sections where students are encouraged to 'help themselves' with their English. We should emphasise that where lists of words or phrases are given in the book, these should not just be studied and learnt out of context, but are intended to be practised and used in speech or writing.

Organisation of *First Certificate Handbook*

The organisation of *First Certificate Handbook* follows that of the three written papers of the First Certificate Examination (see page viii).

Paper 1: Reading Comprehension

All the testing in Paper 1 of the First Certificate Examination is through questions with 'multiple-choice' answers. This is an effective means of assessing comprehension, but tackling multiple-choice questions will not, in itself, help students to read with increased understanding. In this part of the book we suggest ways in which students can

- help themselves to improve their command of words
- understand what they read more clearly
- tackle multiple-choice questions more effectively.

Paper 2: Composition

The aim of this part of the book is to teach structures, words, procedures and skills which will enable students to write compositions of a good standard. Each section contains at least one sample answer written to the level of a good First Certificate candidate – without mistakes, and containing a range of vocabulary and structures that would achieve a good pass in the examination.

Paper 3: Use of English

This part of the book covers areas of English structure and usage which are commonly tested in the examination, and suggests techniques for tackling particular kinds of questions.

Appendices

The three appendices provide material on which students can draw to help them deal with specific problems in a systematic way.

Test Papers

There are three sets of test papers laid out like the First Certificate Examination. The time allotted to each part of the examination has been given at the beginning of each paper, and it is excellent practice to work to this limit. The format of Paper 3 may vary from time to time, and some variety has been put into the test papers to allow for this.

Extract from the University of Cambridge Examination Regulations for 1988

FIRST CERTIFICATE IN ENGLISH

The First Certificate represents a general standard of competence in English at an intermediate level and as an effective basis for further study. It has widespread recognition in commerce and industry, e.g. for public contact or secretarial work in banking, airlines, catering etc., and in individual university faculties, polytechnics and other institutions.

Certificates are awarded in three grades A, B and C on the aggregate of marks gained in the five compulsory papers, with results also in two failing grades D and E.

PAPER 1 Reading Comprehension (1 hour) — 40 marks

  A 25 multiple-choice questions designed to test vocabulary and formal grammatical control, in sentence contexts
  B 15 multiple-choice questions based on three or more texts, designed to test comprehension of gist or detailed content

PAPER 2 Composition (1½ hours) — 40 marks

Two compositions from a choice of descriptive, narrative or discursive topics, including one based on the books listed below.
Assessment is based on organisation and clarity of content, accuracy of grammatical control, fluency and range of expression

PAPER 3 Use of English (2 hours) — 40 marks

Open-completion or transformation items designed to test active control of the language at an appropriate communicative level
Directed writing exercise to test ability to interpret and present information

PAPER 4 Listening Comprehension (approx. 30 minutes) — 20 marks

Questions of varying type (selection, re-ordering, blank-filling etc.) to test accurate understanding of spoken English, based on recorded material

PAPER 5 Interview (approx. 15 minutes) — 40 marks

Based on a picture stimulus, and related passages and other material. The interview may, optionally, be based partly on one of the books listed below, and may be conducted, also optionally, in groups of two or three candidates.

Assessment is based on fluency and grammatical accuracy, pronunciation (individual sounds, and stress and linking of phrases), communicative ability and vocabulary.

△ *Note:* The prescribed books on which the questions in Paper 2 and Paper 5 are based will vary from year to year.

PAPER 1
Reading Comprehension

SECTION A: INTRODUCTION

This section of 25 'multiple-choice' questions is designed by Cambridge to test 'vocabulary and formal grammatical control'. You are required to fill in a blank in a sentence with one of four given words or phrases.

Example:
She quickly washed the milk off the carpet so that it wouldn't leave a _____
A stain **B** colour **C** fault **D** remark
Answer: **A**

The section is intended to test your understanding of which word is correct in a particular context.

General points

It is important to remember that, whatever choice you make, your answer must be correct in both meaning *and* structure (see pages 77–9).

Example 1:
Do you _____ to my smoking a pipe?
A mind **B** excuse **C** object **D** dislike

All these choices seem to express a similar *meaning*, that of 'not liking', but only one is *structurally* correct. Choice **C** (object) is correct because it is followed by 'to': 'mind', 'dislike' and 'excuse' cannot be followed by the word 'to'.

Example 2:
Be careful when you enter the prison. There are some very _____ guard dogs.
A tame **B** friendly **C** beautiful **D** fierce

All these choices are adjectives and would be appropriate from a structural point of view but **A**, **B** and **C** cannot be correct (Why should you be careful of such 'charming' guard dogs?). **D** (fierce) is therefore the right answer.

Example 3:
However hard he tried, he never _____ to swim more than 100 metres.
A succeeded **B** failed **C** realised **D** managed

A (succeeded)	has the right kind of meaning, but is wrong structurally because 'succeed' should be followed by 'in . . . ing'.
B (failed)	is right structurally, but has the wrong meaning (the opposite sense is needed).
C (realised)	is wrong both in meaning and structure.
D (managed)	is correct in meaning and structure ('manage' is followed by 'to').

Remember to read the sentences carefully and check that your choice is correct both in meaning *and* structure.

Specific points

Your aim in preparing for this section is to broaden your understanding of the correct use of English words and phrases. Different ways of doing this are dealt with under six headings.

	page
1 Word and preposition combinations	3
2 Phrasal verbs	4
3 General vocabulary	5
4 Idioms and other common word groups	7
5 Words which cause special difficulties	8
6 Practice and further study	9

To prepare for this part of the examination you must be willing to do a lot of work by yourself, and for the 'self-help' activities suggested below we strongly recommend the use of a good English–English dictionary. It is very important that your dictionary should not only explain the various meanings of words, but should also give clear examples of how they are used.

1 Word and preposition combinations

Example 1:
He was _____ with murder.
A accused **B** arrested **C** charged **D** sentenced
Answer: **C**

Example 2:
She is incapable _____ telling the truth.
A of **B** in **C** at **D** with
Answer: **A**

There are many words in English that are followed by their 'own' preposition. These may be different types of word grammatically – verbs, adjectives or nouns. Some examples are:
   to be fond *of*
   to be safe *from*
   to insist *on*
   to worry *about*
   to find a solution *to*
   to have a preference *for*

The meaning of these combinations is usually clear – the words do not have a 'special' meaning as in the case of phrasal verbs (see page 4). The important thing is that you must *always* learn such words together with their 'own' prepositions: it is useless to learn 'fond' alone, you must learn 'fond of'.

For further study

In Appendix 1 (page 128), you will find a list of many common 'word + preposition' combinations of this kind.

In Appendix 2 (page 130), you will find a further list, this time of 'preposition + word' phrases (e.g. by chance, in time, out of control).

2 Phrasal verbs

Example:
When I was 50 I wanted to start something new, so I took _____ dancing.
A over **B** on **C** up **D** after
Answer: **C**

'Phrasal verb' is a term often used to describe a combination of words, beginning with a verb, which must be understood *together*, rather than as separate words with their normal individual meanings. This is rather different from the verb + preposition combinations where, for example, it was enough to understand the word 'insist' in order to understand 'insist on'. In the phrasal verb example above, your understanding of 'took' and 'up' does not necessarily help you with the meaning of 'took up' (= to begin a new activity or hobby).

Here are two more examples:

Example 1:
I know you're busy, but you'll have to *get round to* doing the garden soon (= finally do it, after a long delay).

Example 2:
We were *making for* the coast (= we were going towards it, going in that direction).

You may know various meanings of the verbs 'get' and 'make', and you probably understand the meanings of the words 'round', 'to' and 'for' in such sentences as 'He flew *round* the world', 'I went *to* London', and 'This is *for* you'. Unfortunately, it is almost impossible to guess the meanings of the phrasal verbs 'get round to' and 'make for' from the meanings of the individual words.

What to do

It is essential for you to build up your stock of phrasal verbs steadily. However, it is unsatisfactory to learn lists of phrasal verbs from books, or to take one verb at a time and find from the dictionary how many phrasal verb combinations it can make (e.g. 'get about', 'get along with', 'get over', 'get round', 'get behind', 'get ahead', 'get away with', etc.). A suggested way of tackling the problem is as follows:

1 Whenever you read a book, newspaper or text in English, get into the habit of *identifying* and underlining phrasal verbs (see page 17 for practice in doing this).

2 Write down in a special notebook the sentences in which they appear.

3 Use your English–English dictionary to look up the meaning, and write this after your sentence.

4 Try to write your own sentence using the same phrasal verb in a different context.

5 Get an English teacher or friend to check that your sentences are correct.

6 Limit the number of new phrasal verbs you collect to, say, two or three each day; if you do five or ten minutes' good work with each, you will quickly build up a useful stock of words which you have actually seen used in the English you have read. This is much more valuable than trying to memorise long lists of words which may (a) be out of date, or (b) mean very little when seen out of context.

3 General vocabulary

Example:
He caught the fish with a _____ made from a pin.
A bow **B** rod **C** hook **D** point
Answer: **C**

To answer some of the questions in Paper 1 Section A you need a good range of general, practical vocabulary.

It is inefficient to try to 'learn' words from a dictionary or vocabulary list, but quite possible to increase your vocabulary by becoming more aware of very common words which you use daily in your own language, but do not know in English.

Here is a suggestion for 'self-help' or 'do-it-yourself' vocabulary building.

What to do

1 Concentrate on one 'theme' for a day or two, for example clothes (40 possible themes are given below, but you can always add some of your own).
2 Use your eyes, ears and imagination to explore the theme. As you dress in the morning, ask yourself questions such as, 'What am I doing now?' and 'Do I know the English words for different parts of my clothes?' In other words, do you know English words such as 'zip', 'belt', 'tights' etc.? If not, are you satisfied to remain in ignorance?
3 Thinking still of your theme and of the words that you do not know, use
   - your bilingual dictionary
   - your English–English dictionary to check on usage
   - any available English speakers to fill in the gaps in your vocabulary.
4 Try to use your new words in your speech or writing.

Suggested themes

Words you may already know	Words you may not know
Clothes dress, sweater, trousers	zip, belt, tights
The human body nose, leg, hand	eyebrow, ankle, elbow
Houses (inside) kitchen, armchair, carpet	kettle, basement, plug
Houses (outside) roof, garden, chimney	drain-pipe, brick, to mow the lawn
The countryside field, river, forest	wood, crops, footpath
Office and factory desk, manager, typist	filing-cabinet, to work overtime, production
School blackboard, teacher, notebook	to punish someone for doing something, ruler, timetable
Roads and streets road, traffic lights, bus stop	pavement, dual carriageway, one-way street
Hospital nurse, doctor, operation	ward, patient, operating theatre
Church priest, to pray, choir	service, to worship, graveyard
Shops and shopping butcher, supermarket, tin	counter, till, newsagent
Food and cooking cooker, to fry, tomato	oven, roast, to stir
Transport car, wheel, railway	container, to tow, boot
Media television, journalist, programme	editor, headline, channel
Relationships father, wife, grandmother	mother-in-law, step-father, nephew

- **Size**
  thin, big, fat — enormous, huge, tiny
- **Degrees of colour**
  red, white, pale blue — faded, dull, bright red
- **Degrees of noise**
  loud, quiet — faint, soft
- **Entertainment**
  cinema, orchestra, theatre — performance, stalls, box-office
- **Free time**
  hobby, go for a walk, restaurant — pub, to play a game, hitch-hiker
- **Sport**
  ball, net, to hit — track-suit, racket, to score a goal
- **Sea and beach**
  sand, wave, shell — high tide, deck-chair, lighthouse
- **Holidays and travel**
  airport, tickets, luggage — travel agent, customs, seasick
- **Crime**
  policeman, detective, thief — clue, witness, sentence
- **Professions and trades**
  doctor, engineer, mechanic — plumber, solicitor, dentist
- **Ways of moving**
  to walk, to run, to jump — to trip over, to limp, to creep
- **Ways of looking**
  to look at, to watch, to see — to stare at, to frown, to glance
- **Ways of taking**
  to hold, to take, to catch — to snatch, to take hold of, to squeeze
- **Verbs associated with nose and mouth**
  to cough, to sneeze, to breathe — to blow your nose, to yawn, to sniff
- **Verbs associated with light**
  to shine, to light — to dazzle, to flash, to glow
- **Verbs associated with liquid**
  to pour, to wash — to drip, to spill, to water the plants
- **Ways of talking**
  to shout, to talk — to whisper, to scream, to chat
- **Verbs associated with small movements**
  to turn, to pull, to push — to bend, to fold, to twist
- **Music**
  singer, pop-music, guitar — to conduct, album, tune
- **Tools**
  hammer, scissors — screwdriver, drill, nail
- **Containers**
  bag, box, packet — parcel, wallet, briefcase
- **Nouns of quantity**
  piece, group, crowd — bunch, loaf, flock
- **Number**
  to count, half, twice — to divide, degree, fraction
- **The weather**
  to rain, cold, wind — to freeze, fog, gale
- **Technology**
  computer, video, hi-fi — calculator, technology, electronic

4 Idioms and other common word groups

Example:
His name was on the _____ of my tongue, but I just couldn't remember it.
A end **B** point **C** tip **D** top

Answer: **C**

'Idiom' is a term often used to describe a group of words which, as in the case of phrasal verbs, must be understood *together* rather than as separate words with their normal individual meanings. Idioms are often used to produce a lively or colourful effect.

Examples:
It was *pouring with rain.* (It was raining a lot)

I'm *up to my eyes in* work. (I've got a lot of work to do)

He's *at a loose end.* (He's unoccupied, he doesn't know what to do)

She's a bit *under the weather.* (She's not feeling very well)

He *jumped at the chance of* going there. (He accepted the opportunity very eagerly)

Besides 'idioms', there are many other common 'sets' of words in English which it is useful for you to recognise and remember. In the examples above, the word groups had 'special' meanings, which often had no connection with the individual meanings of the words used (e.g. 'at a loose end'). In the examples below, the words do not change their meanings when put together; the problem, therefore, is not one of *meaning,* but of *usage:* only one combination is acceptable ('a close friend' is correct, but 'a near friend' is not). Compare the examples:

Correct
- get into the habit of doing something
- give a vivid account of something
- to have no hesitation in doing something
- to settle your affairs
- standard of living

Incorrect
- get into the custom/use of doing something
- give a vivid story/tale/narration of something
- to have no delay/doubt/worry/pause in doing something
- to order/balance/steady/correct your affairs
- grade/state/condition/level of living

What to do

You can improve your knowledge of word groups in the following ways:

- Make a note (in a special notebook) of new expressions you come across in your reading.
- Use an English–English dictionary to find the meaning and usage.
- Limit the number of new expressions to about two or three a day.

5 Words which cause special difficulties

Example:
I couldn't go out before ten o'clock because I was _____ a telephone call from my mother.
A expecting **B** attending **C** waiting **D** hoping

Answer: **A**

There can be different reasons why words cause special difficulties.

- The words are confusing in themselves, either in form or meaning, e.g.
   hard – hardly
   at present – presently
   lie – lay

- A number of English words may have very similar meanings to each other without being completely interchangeable in usage, e.g.
   during – while – for
   opportunity – chance – possibility – occasion
   finally – at last – in the end – eventually

- A word may appear similar to one in your language, but not have exactly the same *meaning* in the two languages, e.g.
   control
   actual
   funny

- A word may have very much the same meaning in English as its translation in your own language, but be *used* in a completely different way, e.g.
   suggest
   let
   travel

There are reference books available which deal specifically with such words, or alternatively a good English–English dictionary will help you.

6 Practice and further study

Below are 50 sentences of the sort commonly found in this part of the examination. First, do the exercise as a *test* (by choosing the word or phrase which best completes each sentence from the four alternatives given). You may then find it useful to study the exercise again, this time checking in your English–English dictionary that you know how to use the 'wrong' words and phrases correctly in a different context.

Exercise 1

1. An umbrella is essential to _____ you from the rain.
   A avoid   B prevent   C protect   D stop

2. I would love to have a house _____.
   A for my own   B of my own   C by my own   D to my own

3. _____ being a brilliant composer he was also a good pianist.
   A Besides   B Beside   C In addition   D As well

4. That noise is _____ me round the bend. Do you think you could stop for a bit?
   A forcing   B driving   C taking   D putting

5. I have very happy _____ of my time in South America.
   A reminders   B remembrances   C souvenirs   D memories

6. I'm looking for a new _____ which will give me better prospects of promotion.
   A work   B employment   C placement   D job

7. The new manager doesn't _____ until next week.
   A overtake   B take over   C take on   D take up

8. When she was younger, her mother wouldn't _____ her play in the street.
   A allow   B permit   C let   D leave

9. The film showed both sides of the argument in order to give a _____ picture of the situation.
   A similar   B alike   C steady   D balanced

10. If you have never _____ the experience of being attacked in the street, you will find it difficult to imagine how unpleasant it can be.
    A got   B had   C done   D made

11. You will never understand my arguments if you don't actually _____ to what I say!
    A listen   B hear   C understand   D appreciate

12. What is your _____ of my new tie? Don't you think the colours match my shirt rather well?
    A meaning   B intention   C mind   D opinion

13. Her upbringing was very _____; she was never allowed out of the house in the evenings.
    A strict   B grave   C strong   D liberal

14. What's the correct _____ from here to town by bus?
    A rent   B tax   C fare   D fee

15. That's precisely what I mean. You've hit the _____ on the head.
    A pin   B nail   C point   D idea

16. Put your money in your pocket, _____ you might lose it.
    A in case   B unless   C otherwise   D if

17. I can't give you both a lift – my car only _____ two people.
    A bears   B holds   C contains   D has

18. The team manager _____ his players for not trying hard enough.
    A blamed   B accused   C attacked   D criticised

19. I was unwilling to sign the agreement _____ I was completely satisfied with all the conditions.
    A until   B because   C after   D then

20. If you want to return the sweater, you must bring the _____ with you as proof of purchase.
    A note   B recipe   C receipt   D prescription

21. Oh hello, you've changed your hairstyle. I didn't _____ you.
    A realise   B remark   C watch   D recognise

22. You don't get many _____ for skiing in the south of England.
    A possibilities   B opportunities   C chance   D occasion

23. It's quite common for luggage to be _____ at the Customs.
    A tested   B controlled   C checked   D overseen

24. There's no _____ to cry just because you have spilt the milk!
    A use   B need   C point   D purpose

25 He doesn't mean to hurt people, but he's so tactless that he _____ to upset them without realising what he's done.
A tends B succeeds C likes D comes

26 Out there on the islands, things move at rather a slow _____.
A time B step C way D pace

27 _____ it was such a rainy day, we all stayed at home and played cards rather than go out.
A Despite B For C Since D However

28 I'm afraid I won't be able to give you an answer on the _____; I'll have to ask the manager first.
A dot B spot C moment D point

29 It's a very tricky problem, but if you leave it with me for a few days, I'll _____ it.
A look forward to B look into C look down D look across

30 He searched the interior of the car thoroughly for the ring he had dropped: unfortunately he never thought of looking _____.
A under B underneath C inside D above

31 The cost of a full meal was only a _____ more than we had paid for a cup of coffee.
A little B lot C few D much

32 Sooner or later you will have to _____ up to the problem of finding a replacement.
A make B meet C come D face

33 Mr Titmarsh had a very _____ escape from death on his way to work.
A near B fine C narrow D just

34 'I am absolutely _____ to eliminate all poverty, injustice, unhappiness and crime from our society in the next five years,' said the new president.
A intended B wanted C succeeded D determined

35 Let's take our umbrellas with us just in _____ it rains.
A the case of B case C case of D the case that

36 Please leave the machine in good _____ when you have finished using it.
A condition B conditions C use D work

37 Her best friend lived in a house _____, so she was never without a playmate.
A near B next C nearby D nearest

38 The minister visited the new stadium _____ and then went on to the town hall.
A soon B shortly C presently D briefly

39 The standard of living has _____ quite a lot in most countries over the past twenty years.
A risen B raised C lifted D raised up

40 A(n) _____ mistake which many students make is to leave out the preposition.
A ordinary B common C plain D just

41 On no _____ must you press that button! Arrghhh . . .
A circumstances B time C reason D account

42 Since Cecil always fainted at the sight of blood, it was quite _____ to all his friends that he would never be a successful doctor.
A understood B obvious C right D easy

43 I was so sure that it was a mushroom and not poisonous that I had no _____ in eating it.
A hesitation B hurry C delay D pause

44 All the seats in the theatre were _____ three weeks before the performance.
A preserved B engaged C occupied D reserved

45 I wouldn't go there, not for all the _____!
A coffee in Brazil B tea in China C fish in the sea D rain in England

46 He's never been a(n) _____ person, but he's never been as late as this before.
A accurate B punctual C strict D certain

47 When we finally _____ to the top of the mountain, we found another peak rising in front of us.
A arrived B reached C got D attained

48 It's important to _____ the instructions printed at the back of the book.
A pay attention to B take care of C care for D look after

49 There must be a(n) _____ of at least three metres between the desks in the examination room.
A place B room C space D expanse

50 Turn the book round, you've got it _____.
A downside up B upside down C inside out D outside in

SECTION B: INTRODUCTION

Multiple-choice questions, based on three or more texts, designed to test your ability to understand the general meaning and the details of what you read.

The aim of this section is to help you to read with greater ease and greater accuracy, and subsequently to answer questions more systematically.

The section is divided into three:

		page
1	Finding the meaning of unknown words	12
2	Reading with clear comprehension	20
3	Dealing with multiple-choice questions on written texts.	23

1 Finding the meaning of unknown words

It is important to develop a technique for deducing the meanings of unknown words and phrases, where they are essential to the understanding of a passage. A step-by-step technique is suggested below.

Step 1: Decide what function or purpose the word or phrase has in the sentence

It is not necessary to know or use grammatical expressions for this, although for convenience some are introduced below. What is important is to see clearly how the word which you do not know *works* in the sentence.

Example 1:
Study the following sentences, with their comments about the work of the words in bold type.

1 There was a **bangle** on her wrist; it was made of gold.
   The word 'a' tells us that 'bangle' is a *noun*, or substantive (that is, a person, thing, etc.); and 'it' and 'gold' make it clear that it is a *thing*.

2 The **adjutant** walked into the officers' sitting-room: he sat down and ordered a large whisky.
   'The' means that the word is again a *noun*. 'He', together with 'walked' and 'sat', suggests that it must be a *person*.

3 'I won't have any supper, thanks. I've been feeling a bit **queasy** all day.'
   'Queasy' must be an *adjective* (a word that describes a person, thing, etc.). Here it describes 'I'.

4 He very **brusquely** interrupted my conversation.
   'Brusquely' describes the way in which he did something; it would be described as an *adverb*. Many adverbs describing how something is done end in -ly in English.

5 He **sauntered** along the street.
   'Sauntered' ends in '-ed', and follows 'he': it must therefore be a *verb* in the past tense.

6 'I don't like the way you **lounge** in that chair!'
   'Lounge' follows 'you', and so is probably a *verb*; this time there is no 'ending' (such as '-ed' or '-ing'), which means that if it is a verb it is in the simple present tense.

7 'I wonder what there is **beyond** those hills?'
   From its position before 'those hills', 'beyond' must be a *preposition of 'place'*.

Example 2:
Each of the following sentences contain the word 'wungle', which is a nonsense word with no meaning in English. In each sentence it is used in a different way, and is clearly a different kind of word. Look carefully at each one to see the different language 'function' it performs. At the same time, try to think of a simple word which you could put in the place of 'wungle' in each sentence – e.g. 'man' in sentence 1, or 'disappointment' in sentence 7.

1 I stopped a wungle in the street and asked him the way to the Post Office. (Noun – person)
2 We paid to go into the zoo and see the wungles. (Noun – animal/bird/insect)
3 The earth in my garden is so rich that my wungles are growing very nicely. (Noun – plant)
4 I took the heavy metal wungle out of its box. (Noun – thing)
5 She walked into the wungle and up the stairs. (Noun – place)
6 It was made of wungle. (Noun – substance)
7 The experience gave me a strong feeling of wungle. (Noun – abstract)
8 We visited Wungle last year. (Noun – name of person/place)
9 They saw not just one, but a whole wungle of them. (Noun – collective)
10 She is a very wunglible lady. (Adjective)
11 He was unfortunately rather wungled last night. (Adjective – 'negative')
12 I am pleased that it was all so wungleful. (Adjective – 'positive')
13 He was wungily dressed. (Adverb)
14 Congratulations on doing it so wunglefully. (Adverb – 'psitive')
15 We were disappointed at how wungily they treated us. (Adverb – 'negative')
16 People often wungle things they don't like. (Verb – transitive)
17 She spends every Saturday night at home, wungling. (Verb – intransitive)

Look in your grammar book and dictionary to make sure that you fully understand the grammatical terms such as 'intransitive verb' and 'abstract noun' which are used above.

READING COMPREHENSION

Exercise 2

When you have studied the sentences above, look at the different parts played by the nonsense word 'sprill' below; in each case describe what *kind* of word it is, and say why.

1. I'm glad to see you looking so sprill today.
2. Scientists used to visit the island in large numbers to study the many kinds of sprills living there.
3. The children were sprilling in the playground.
4. I met a very friendly sprill the other day, and we had a nice chat.
5. It was such a sprilling film that it kept us all on the edge of our seats.
6. He began to talk sprillily about their journey.
7. I sprill him every time I see him.
8. Sprill is cheap and easy to get to for holidays.
9. He was a sprill man with long hair and short legs.
10. I enjoyed visiting the local sprill yesterday.
11. Everybody is capable of sprill.
12. Ugh! What's that? Sprill?
13. Unfortunately it was done very sprillily, and nobody was really satisfied.
14. What's Sprill doing here? He should be at work!
15. You'll soon have to count them not singly, but in sprills.

Exercise 3

Now look at each of the sentences in Exercise 2 again, and try to write down three real words which could replace the word 'sprill' in each sentence. Be sure that the words you write have the grammatical function that you wrote down in each case when you did Exercise 2.

Example:
Sentence 1. Happy, well, smart, pleased, friendly, etc.

Exercise 4

In each of the following sentences one word is omitted, and a gap is left in its place. Think what *kind* of word should fill the gap in each case, then write down two possible words for each sentence. (If you find this difficult, look back to *Example 1* and *Example 2* on page 12.) The first sentence has been done for you.

1. I hate _____ who speak rudely to me.
   Answer: noun – person; Englishmen, children, etc.
2. He was _____ along the street, singing to himself.
3. He opened the door very _____.
4. As soon as she opened the door, I _____ her.
5. He was a very _____ man of fifty-three.
6. Pass me that _____, please.
7. She is not a person with much _____ in her life.
8. The forest was full of _____, which ran away when we approached.
9. It was an absolutely _____ day, one which I wish to forget as quickly as possible.
10. More and more of them arrived, until by four o'clock there was a large _____ of them in front of us.
11. I'm afraid I don't like _____ much; he never seems interested in what I have to say to him.
12. The floor was covered in _____; I wondered whose job it would be to clear it up.
13. At three o'clock in the morning there was a loud _____ which woke many of us up.
14. They entertained us _____ all evening, and we went home happy.
15. What a _____ girl she is! I really would like to meet her again!

Step 2: Look at the context of the unknown word

The 'context' of a word is its 'surroundings' – all the words before and after it, not necessarily only those in the same sentence. The context will nearly always give many clues and hints about the meaning of the unknown word. You have already seen that deciding what work the word does in the sentence can quite often give some idea of its meaning; the aim now is to get even nearer to the meaning by gathering any other available information which can help. Look at these words:

grip	badger	wriggle
cobbler	gloomily	greasy
jack	soggy	shriek
tuck	totter	dimly
puddle	dunce	glum
relief	cuddle	thrush

Most of these words are probably unknown to you when they stand alone, but when they are seen in the context of a sentence, as below, it is easy to see what they mean:

- I *gripped* the wheel as hard as I could with both hands, and began to turn it.
  'Grip' must be a verb meaning 'hold' or 'take hold of'.
- The *cobbler* had just finished repairing my shoes when I went into his little shop.
  A 'cobbler' must be a man who repairs shoes.
- I put the *jack* under the car, and turned the handle until two of the car's wheels were off the ground.
  A 'jack' must be a tool or instrument used for raising the wheels of a car from the ground.

 Exercise 5

Write a similar short explanation for the words in italics in the following sentences, deducing the meanings from the contexts:

1. The *badger* slowly moved out from the trees into the open ground; we could see its black and white head clearly in the moonlight.
2. 'It's no use,' he admitted *gloomily*, 'I shall never be able to do it.'
3. Someone had spilt a whole cup of tea over my bread, which was now *soggy* and impossible to eat.
4. When he heard his enemies looking for him, he *wriggled* back carefully and quietly into the leaves.
5. The waiter took their order; he looked hot and *greasy*, as if the cook had fried him with the food.
6. A sudden *shriek* of horror from outside the door caused me to drop the egg on the floor.
7. *Tuck* your shirt inside your trousers; it looks most untidy hanging out like that.
8. He stepped back, fell over the dog, and sat down in a large *puddle*: his trousers were wet through.
9. I felt a strong sense of *relief* when that weekend was over. It was as if all my problems and worries had suddenly been removed.
10. Almost exhausted, he *tottered* the last few metres to the finish, and fell into the arms of his waiting friends.
11. I felt a real *dunce*, because I had understood nothing and written nothing by the time all the others in the class had finished the question.
12. The little girl *cuddled* her doll lovingly as she lay in bed.
13. I found it very difficult to see what I was eating in the *dimly*-lit restaurant.
14. Don't look so *glum*! Things may get better!
15. I was woken by the sound of a *thrush* singing from a branch on the tree outside my bedroom window.

 Exercise 6

In this exercise, replace the word printed in italics in each sentence with a word you know which would be suitable.

1. I stopped a *kachina* in the street and asked him the way to the Chinese restaurant.
2. The front of his *tunicle* was covered in week-old egg, and he looked extremely dirty.
3. We paid to go into the zoo to see the *bunyips*.
4. How many more *torgochs* are you going to catch? I'm cold and wet, and I'm beginning to feel a little seasick.
5. When you get into the park, please don't pick the *kawakawas*.
6. *Fulmars* can be seen in their hundreds in May, sitting on their eggs or flying over the sea looking for fish.
7. Because it is made entirely of *blunge*, our product is stronger but lighter than anything similar.
8. There was some kind of *razzia* at the nurses' home last night; everyone is very angry about it.
9. I haven't seen a *quaich* like that before. What is it used for?
10. When we entered the *vomitory* we immediately felt the warmth of the central heating.
11. The three fat ladies sitting in the *tumtum* looked extremely uncomfortable.
12. *Obmutescence* is not a very good quality if found in a Prime Minister or a car salesman.
13. I fell asleep and missed the most important part of his talk. Now I'll have to wait at least another *saros* for an opportunity to hear it.
14. Do you believe in the theory of *sandhi*?

15 I'm sure you're right to travel as much as possible while you're here. *Penrhyndeudraeth* is lovely at this time of the year.

16 I'm worried! It's only showing fifty *torrs*!

17 The garden isn't very big, only about three *perches*.

18 I don't mind a few at a time, but I think a whole *quire* is rather too much.

19 He was pleased that it had been so *pukkah*.

20 I'm sorry I was *agamic* yesterday.

21 Why do you always have to be so *thrawn*?

22 How would I describe it? Well, it was *turdoid*, and . . .

23 I was completely *sherardised* by the day's activities, and I still don't really feel well.

24 How did you manage to do it so *slickly*? I think you're wonderful!

25 Can't you behave a little less *operosely*?

26 Against the wishes of his people he married *morganatically*.

27 People often *ballyrag* what they don't understand.

28 When he *ponced* into the room, everybody looked up in surprise.

29 I could see him out in the garden, *troating*.

30 *Ochone*! What can I do?

  Exercise 7

Read the following text once, and then look carefully at each of the words printed in italics. Remember when looking at each word (if its meaning is unknown to you) that you should decide:

- what kind of word it is

- what information is given in the sentence or the whole passage which can help you to work out the meaning.

We got in a little blue car heavily decorated with shining *brass* and upholstered in deep red plush: we were the only ones in a car made to take six. As we waited to start, I tried to make myself comfortable on the seats, but they were (5) so high and *vast* that I could only sit on the edge with my legs *dangling* and my hands tightly *clutching* the brass safety *rail* in front: I felt like a pea in a pod. The operator pulled a greasy *lever* and the little car, after a sudden *jerk*, (10) slowly began to climb the noisy ratchet railway to the top. We passed huge, *wobbling* wheels, and lots of other very oily machinery.

The machinery was making a dreadful *din*. I *peeped* over the side of the car – all South (15) Shields seemed to be gathered round the Wouldhave Memorial, watching our ascent. As we *crawled* higher and higher my spirits sank lower and lower. Below us, some seagulls were flying about among the *struts*: after that, I did (20) not dare look over the edge of the car again.

From *The Only Child* by James Kirkup

When you have done this, look at the questions which follow and in each case write down from the four choices given, the word which seems *closest* in meaning to the word quoted from the passage.

1 brass (line 2)
 A cloth
 B wood
 C paper
 D metal

2 vast (line 6)
  A small
  B hard
  C big
  D soft
3 dangling (line 7)
  A running
  B hanging
  C moving
  D standing
4 clutching (line 8)
  A touching
  B holding
  C feeling
  D tasting
5 rail (line 8)
  A door
  B net
  C exit
  D bar
6 lever (line 10)
  A machine
  B wheel
  C button
  D handle
7 jerk (line 10)
  A movement
  B sound
  C explosion
  D light
8 wobbling (line 12)
  A moving
  B speeding
  C hurting
  D stopping
9 din (line 14)
  A product
  B movement
  C thing
  D noise
10 peeped (line 15)
  A fell
  B went
  C looked
  D spoke
11 crawled (line 18)
  A moved
  B fell
  C started
  D wanted
12 struts (line 20)
  A people
  B supports
  C feelings
  D water

Exercise 8

Now do the same with this text.

Again, read the text carefully and then decide for yourself what meanings the words in italics probably have *before* looking at the possible meanings which are given.

Choose only *one* of the possible meanings given.

Jack was bent double. He was down like a sprinter, his nose only a few inches from the humid earth. The tree trunks and the creepers that hung from them lost themselves in a green dusk thirty feet above him; and all around was the undergrowth. There was only the *faintest* indication of a trail here; a cracked twig and the impression of one side of an animal's hoof. He lowered his chin and stared at the *traces* as though he would force them to speak to him. Then dog-like, uncomfortably on all fours yet *unheeding* his discomfort, he *stole* forward five yards and stopped. (5) (10)

Jack *crouched* with his face a few inches away from this clue, then stared forward into the semi-darkness of the undergrowth. His sandy hair, considerably longer than it had been when they dropped in, was lighter now; and his bare back was a mass of dark freckles and peeling sunburn. A sharpened stick about five feet long trailed from his right hand; and except for a pair of *tattered* shorts held up by his knife-belt he was naked. He closed his eyes, raised his head and breathed in gently, assessing the current of warm air for information. The forest and he were very still.
   At length he let out his breath in a long sigh and opened his eyes. They were bright blue, eyes that in this frustration seemed nearly mad. He passed his tongue across dry lips and *scanned* the uncommunicative forest. Then again he stole forward and *cast* this way and that over the ground. (15) (20) (25) (30)

Adapted from *Lord of the Flies* by William Golding

READING COMPREHENSION

1 faintest (line 6)
  A biggest
  B brightest
  C best
  D smallest
2 traces (line 9)
  A pigs
  B leaves
  C insects
  D signs
3 unheeding (line 12)
  A complaining about
  B looking at
  C not paying attention to
  D undoing
4 stole (line 12)
  A ran noisily
  B robbed
  C moved quietly
  D took

5 crouched (line 14)
  A kept still with his legs bent
  B moved forwards with his eyes open
  C walked backwards with his arms out
  D lay down with his hands behind his head
6 tattered (line 22)
  A smart
  B repaired
  C destroyed
  D torn
7 scanned (line 31)
  A photographed
  B stared at
  C listened
  D looked for
8 cast (line 32)
  A threw
  B jumped
  C ran
  D searched

Exercise 9

This exercise and Exercise 10 will give you more practice in finding the meaning of unknown words. Now, however, rather than looking at single words, you will be trying to decide the meaning of phrasal verbs, idioms, and other groups of words.

The first problem is to *recognise* such 'sets' of words. (Earlier in this section, on page 4, it was suggested that one way to increase your knowledge of phrasal verbs and idioms was to recognise and underline them in your own reading. Look back at pages 3–7 to remind yourself of the kind of expressions we are referring to.)

Now look at the following passage and notice how the words in italics must be understood together rather than as individual words. Then try to suggest a meaning in your own words for these phrases: the first one has been done for you as an example.

The Norwegian government is *doing its best* to keep the oil industry under control. A new law limits exploration to an area south of the southern end of the long coastline; production limits *have been laid down* and oil companies have not been allowed to employ more than a limited number of foreign workers. But the oil industry has a way of *getting over* such problems, and few people believe that the government will be able to *hold things back* for long. As one Norwegian politician said last week: 'We will soon be changed *beyond all recognition*'.

1 'doing its best' = the government is trying as hard as it can.
2 'have been laid down' =
3 'getting over' =
4 'hold things back' =
5 'beyond all recognition' =

17

PAPER 1

Exercise 10

Here, as in Exercise 9, the questions require your understanding of phrasal verbs and idioms, not just individual words.

Remember to look at each group of words in italics as if it were one 'idea', and decide what meaning you think it has before choosing *one* of the three possible meanings given.

Mr Moggerhanger *fixed me up with* an attic room at his big house in Ealing. My quarters, as he called them, were a room with a sloping ceiling against which I continually bumped my head, unless I *went around doubled up* like a collier. (5) There were a few oddments and throwouts of furniture *spaced about*, which were enough for me. The floor was bare boards, covered with jagged splashes of white paint where some maniac had decorated the walls and *let flip with* (10) *it* everywhere.

As soon as I got there Moggerhanger told me to take out the Bentley and drive it around for an hour to *get the feel of it*. It was like driving somebody's living-room. You could almost (15) stand up inside it, and *touch it along* at over a hundred miles an hour when you dared. I had no other thought in my head when I'd *lifted off* except to keep it unscratched and *in one piece*. My main aim was to have it out on the A4 and (20) into the country, because I didn't want to *run it against* too much traffic on my first *hand-in*. I acted gingerly, until I found that its acceleration and speed, not to mention its presence, overawed most other drivers. All I had to do (25) was *flash straight for* a souped-up sales rep. in his new Cortina as if I were intent on smashing him to bits, and he'd get out of the way sooner or later. Sometimes it was later, but he slid from my path nevertheless. The only danger was (30) those people with foreign cars, owner-occupiers who were so convinced of their superiority over anything English that they were insane or fanatic enough not to *get clear* under any circumstances, and in that case I had to *pull* (35) *back*. But I didn't hate them for this, for in many ways they were right not to *give in* just because I drove a Bentley, which was after all somebody else's.

From *A Start in Life* by Alan Sillitoe

READING COMPREHENSION

1. fixed me up with (line 1)
   A connected me with
   B arranged for me to live in
   C took me down to
2. went around (line 5)
   A went to the room
   B walked around the house
   C moved when in the room
3. doubled up (line 5)
   A with a friend
   B bending
   C climbing
4. spaced about (line 7)
   A approximately
   B carefully measured
   C scattered around the room
5. let flip with it (lines 10–11)
   A carefully painted it
   B turned it over
   C allowed it to make a mess
6. get the feel of it (line 14)
   A find out what it was like to drive
   B find out where he was supposed to go
   C control the car
7. touch it along (line 16)
   A drive it
   B touch it
   C run along it
8. lifted off (line 18)
   A taken it off
   B lifted
   C started driving
9. in one piece (line 19)
   A peaceful
   B undamaged
   C in my room
10. run it against (lines 21–2)
    A crash into
    B meet while driving
    C drive fast from
11. hand-in (line 22)
    A money for a car
    B present of a car
    C experimental drive in the car
12. flash straight for (line 26)
    A drive directly towards
    B walk towards
    C have a drink with
13. get clear (line 34)
    A get out of the way
    B find out the details
    C explain
14. pull back (lines 35–6)
    A change direction or speed
    B close the door of the car
    C go backwards
15. give in (line 37)
    A give me their cars
    B attack me
    C allow me to win

2 Reading with clear comprehension

In the next three exercises the texts are followed by questions which help you to check if you are reading carefully enough. *You should read each text at least twice, slowly and carefully, before you look at the questions.*

Each text is followed first by three general comprehension questions, to be answered in your own words. It should not be necessary to look back at the text you have just read while answering the questions; if it *is* necessary, you probably needed to read the text more slowly, or more carefully, or more often.

In the second set of exercises after each text you must decide whether the sentences you are given are 'right' or 'wrong'. 'Right' means that the sentence gives some information which is almost exactly the same as something you have read in the text. 'Wrong' means that the sentence contains information which is different in some way from what you have read (even though some of the same words may be used).

While working through this second set of questions, it *will* probably be necessary to look back and read again very carefully those sections of the text to which the sentences refer.

 Exercise 11   slip off – leave

We got to Waterloo Station at eleven, and asked where the eleven-five started from. Of course nobody knew; nobody at Waterloo ever does know where a train is going to start from, or where it is going to when it does start, or (5) anything about it. The porter who took our things thought it would go from number two platform, while another porter, with whom we discussed the question, had heard it said that it would go from number one. The station-master, (10) on the other hand, was certain that it would start from number four.

To put an end to the matter, we went upstairs, and asked the traffic manager, and he told us that he had just met a man, who said (15) that he had seen it at number three platform. We went there, and were told that the train waiting there was believed to be the Southampton express.

Then our porter said that he thought that he (20) recognised the train standing at another platform. Away we went again, and saw the engine-driver, and asked him if he was going to Kingston. He said that he wasn't sure, but he thought he was. We slipped half a crown into (25) his hand, and begged him to be the eleven-five for Kingston.

'Nobody will ever know, on this line,' we said, 'what you are, or where you are going. You know the way, so slip off quietly and go to (30) Kingston.'

'Well, I don't really know,' replied the noble fellow, 'but I suppose some train has got to go to Kingston; and I'll do it.'

Thus we got to Kingston by the London and (35) South-Western Railway.

We learnt, afterwards, that the train we had come by was really the Exeter mail, and that they had spent hours at Waterloo looking for it and nobody knew what had become of it. (40)

From *Three Men in a Boat* by Jerome K. Jerome

General questions about the passage
1 What did they want to find out at Waterloo Station?
2 Who were the different people they asked for information?
3 How did they eventually get to their destination? by trick

READING COMPREHENSION

Right or wrong?

Example 1:
Eleven people arrived at Waterloo Station.

Answer: Wrong.... ('at eleven' means at eleven o'clock; it has no connection with the number of people.)

Example 2:
It is difficult to get accurate information about trains at Waterloo.

Answer: Right.... (Nobody at Waterloo according to the passage ever does know where a train will start from, or where it is going to when it does start, or anything about it.)

Now say whether each of the following statements is right or wrong:

1. No trains ever start from Waterloo.
2. The train they wanted was definitely supposed to leave from number four platform.
3. All the people they asked said different things.
4. None of the people they asked was sure that the information he gave was accurate.
5. The traffic manager had seen the train at number three platform.
6. The train in which they went to Kingston was not really the Kingston train.
7. The Exeter mail train did not go to Exeter that day.
8. The train they went on left from number five platform.
9. They paid the engine driver to take them where they wanted to go.
10. They went on the Southampton express.

Exercise 12

Old Thompson was seventy-four the winter his wife died. She was sixty-nine. They would have celebrated their golden wedding the following summer and they were a quiet and fond couple.

Bob, the Thompsons' younger son, and his (5) wife Annie were living in the house in Dover Street when Mrs Thompson died. The Thompsons had had four children. The elder son was lost at sea during the war; a daughter married and went to Australia, and a second (10) daughter, Maud, fifteen years older than Bob, lived with her family in another part of the town.

Bob and Annie had not known each other long before they became eager to get married: (15) Bob because he wanted Annie and she (though she was fond of Bob in her own way) because she could at last see a life away from her coarse family. When Mrs Thompson suggested that they marry and live with them in Dover Street (20) until they could get a house of their own, Annie hesitated. Her idea of marriage had been to gain a husband and an orderly, well-furnished home at the same time. But she soon saw the advantages in this arrangement. She would, first (25) of all, escape from her present life into a house which was quiet and efficiently managed, even if it were not hers; and she would be able to go on working so that she and Bob could save up even more quickly for their own house. She (30) would also get Bob, a good enough husband for any working-class girl; he was kind and pliable, ready to be bent her way whenever it was necessary for her intentions.

In time Bob became used to the silent figure (35) in the house; but Annie, who since her mother-in-law's death had left her job and was at home all day, began to find the old man's constant presence a source of growing annoyance. (40)

From *Waiting* by Stan Barstow

General questions

1. Why did Annie hesitate about going to live in Dover Street?
2. What three considerations made her finally decide to go there?
3. Who was 'the silent figure in the house'?

Right or wrong?

1 The Thompsons had been married for forty-nine years when Mrs Thompson died.
2 Annie was working when she married.
3 Annie's idea of the perfect marriage was to have not only a husband, but also a house of their own.
4 Mr Thompson had four children living when his wife died.
5 Annie enjoyed her home life before she got married.
6 Bob was a strong husband who would always make the decisions in his own home.
7 Annie was annoyed by old Thompson from the moment she moved into his house.
8 Old Thompson married when he was about twenty-five years old.
9 Annie did not expect that she and Bob would always live with his parents.
10 The Thompsons were a coarse family.
11 Annie came from a working-class family.

 ## Exercise 13

To understand the next passage you need to know that a 'will', or 'last will and testament' is a written statement saying how a person wants his money or possessions to be distributed when he is dead.

The ideas here seem very complicated at first, but should become clear if you read with great care, perhaps three or even four times.

'Many years before her death, Lady Dormer made a will. Her husband and daughter were then dead, and Henry Dormer had left money to his relations, who were therefore rich. He had also left seven hundred thousand pounds (5) to his wife, Lady Dormer, and she divided her money as follows. Twelve thousand pounds were to go to Miss Ann Dorland. All the rest was to go to her brother, General Fentiman, if he was still alive at her death. But if he should (10) die before her, most of the money was to go to Miss Ann Dorland, and fifteen thousand pounds were to be equally divided between Major Robert Fentiman and his brother, George.'
   Wimsey whistled softly. (15)
   'I quite agree with you,' said Mr Murbles. 'It is a most awkward situation. Lady Dormer died at exactly 10.37 a.m. on November 11th. General Fentiman died that same morning at some time, probably after ten o'clock, which (20) was his usual hour for arriving at the Club, and certainly before 7 p.m., when his death was discovered. If he died immediately on his arrival, or at any time up to 10.36, then Miss Dorland receives a lot of money and the (25) Fentiman brothers get only about seven thousand pounds each. But if his death took place even a few seconds after 10.37, Miss Dorland receives only twelve thousand pounds. The old General, in the short time between the (30) deaths, received the rest, and so we must follow his wishes as shown in his will. Therefore George Fentiman gets the small amount left to him by his grandfather's will; but Robert – who, as you remember, receives what is left – gets (35) more than half a million pounds.'

From *The Unpleasantness at the Bellona Club* by Dorothy L. Sayers

General questions

1 Who are the two people who have died, and when did they die?
2 The great problem here is one of *time*. What exactly must be found out to resolve the difficulty?
3 Who are the two people *most* concerned to know the answer to the problem mentioned above?

Right or wrong?

1 Lady Dormer was a rich woman.
2 Henry Dormer left all his money to General Fentiman.
3 If General Fentiman died before Lady Dormer, Robert Fentiman gets more money than if Lady Dormer died first.
4 If General Fentiman died at 10.15, Miss Dorland will be rich.
5 If General Fentiman died at 10.38, George Fentiman will be rich.
6 General Fentiman left by far the greater part of his money to Robert Fentiman.
7 George gets £7,500 if General Fentiman died at 10.35.
8 It is not known precisely when Lady Dormer died.
9 General Fentiman probably did not die after 10 o'clock.
10 Robert Fentiman has a very good reason for hoping that General Fentiman died after Lady Dormer.
11 Lady Dormer was General Fentiman's sister.

3 Dealing with multiple-choice questions on written texts

When four possible answers to a question are given, it is easy to forget the obvious fact that *three of the answers are wrong*.

It is important that you should understand the text *before* looking at the questions and answers. If you look at the possible answers first, you may misread the text because of having three pieces of inaccurate or distracting information in your mind.

1. Read each of the following short passages very slowly and carefully two or three times and decide *exactly* what has been said.

2. Then look at the question which follows each passage, and think how you would answer it *in your own words*.

3. Look at the four possible answers given, and decide which of them corresponds most closely to your answer.

4. Finally, check that the answer you have chosen really does contain only information from the passage. (Make sure that you have not let your own ideas or imagination influence your choice.)

Example:
She left home not so much because she was unhappy, but because she wanted to live independently; and although she found that living alone had its ups and downs, she was on the whole happier.

How did she feel about living alone?
A Unhappy B Very happy C More satisfied
D Lonely

1. Read the above passage two or three times. You should then be able to understand how she felt about living at home, why she left, and how she felt about living on her own.

2. Now try to answer the question 'How did she feel about living alone?' in your own words.
   There were some good things and some bad things, but she felt happier than she had felt at home.

3. Now look at the four multiple-choice questions. Remember only *one* is correct. Which of them is nearest to your *own* answer?

A Unhappy. — No, not always – some things were better.
B Very happy. — No, not always – some things were worse.
C More satisfied. — Yes I think so, but I'll just check D first.
D Lonely. — No, at least we're not told that she felt lonely, only that she lived alone, which is not the same.

4. Check the passage again to make sure your choice is right.
   Did she really feel more satisfied about living alone?
   Yes, it says 'she was on the whole happier'.
   Okay. C is the answer.

Now follow the same four-step procedure for the following three exercises.

Exercise 14

As a method of heating a house, gas fires are probably as effective as anything short of full central heating. Although perhaps less attractive than coal fires, they have the great advantage of convenience; and they are certainly more economical than electric fires.

What are the good things about gas fires?
A They are the most effective way of heating a house
B They are less expensive than coal fires
C They are more attractive than electric fires
D They are generally better than both coal and electric fires

PAPER 1

Exercise 15

One of the joys of being a farmer must be the outdoor life that he leads. He may have to be out at all times and in all weathers, but compared with a factory worker, who spends his eight hours bending over noisy machinery, the farmer must lead an incredibly healthy life.

What is a farmer's life like?
A Probably healthier than a factory worker's
B He must always be outside
C He never bends over noisy machinery
D He is incredibly healthy

Exercise 16

When Mr Essex surveyed the scene of destruction in his office that morning, he reflected that the one bright spot in the whole affair was the fact that his insurance premium had been renewed the day before. Had he been able to see the stamped but unposted letter lying beneath his overturned desk, he might well have been rather less happy.

How did Mr Essex feel?
A Happy to be in that spot
B Unhappy that his insurance renewal had not actually been posted
C Unhappy, but glad about the insurance
D Less happy than he would have been if he could have seen the letter

Further practice

Finally, here are six passages of reading comprehension followed by multiple-choice questions. In the First Certificate examination you may have to answer questions on passages which have been chosen because they illustrate different styles of writing in English. These may be:

- fictional (e.g. a narrative, like Exercise 17)
- non-fictional (like Exercise 21)
- 'functional' (i.e. taken from instructions, notices or advertisements like Exercise 20)

On the basis of the work done in this section, here is a suggested systematic procedure for reading a text and answering questions on it. The procedure is the same whatever kind of passage it is you have to read.

Step
1 Read through the text once for general comprehension.
2 Read again, and work out possible meanings for those words you do not know.
3 Read again, slowly and carefully, trying to get a clear picture of exactly what has been said in the passage.
4 If necessary, read the passage once more to understand more complicated or confusing ideas.
5 Look at each question in turn (as far as possible avoid looking too closely at the suggested answers), and decide how you might answer it *in your own words*.
6 Look at the various answers offered and choose the one which you think fits best.
7 Check the answers you have chosen by looking back again to the relevant parts of the text.

After the first text, some questions have been answered for you to illustrate this procedure.

Exercise 17

During the past few years, Mr Boggis had achieved considerable fame among his friends in the trade by his ability to produce unusual and often quite rare items with astonishing regularity. Apparently the man had a source of supply that was almost inexhaustible, a sort of private warehouse, and it seemed that all he had to do was to drive out to it once a week and help himself. Whenever they asked him where he got the stuff, he would smile knowingly and wink and murmur something about a little secret.

The idea behind Mr Boggis's little secret was a simple one, and it had come to him as a result of something that had happened on a certain Sunday afternoon nearly nine years before, while he was driving in the country.

He had gone out in the morning to visit his old mother, who lived in Sevenoaks, and on the way back the fanbelt on his car had broken, causing the engine to overheat and the water to boil away. He had got out of the car and walked to the nearest house, a smallish farm building about fifty yards off the road, and had asked the woman who answered the door if he could please have a jug of water.

While he was waiting for her to fetch it, he happened to glance in through the door of the living-room, and there, not five yards from where he was standing, he spotted something that made him so excited the sweat began to come out all over the top of his head. It was a large oak armchair of a type that he had only seen once before in his life. Each arm, as well as the panel at the back, was supported by a row of eight beautifully turned spindles. The back panel itself was decorated by an inlay of the most delicate floral design, and the head of a duck was carved to lie along half the length of either arm. Good God, he thought. This thing is late fifteenth century!

He poked his head in further through the door, and there, by heavens, was another of them on the other side of the fire-place!

He couldn't be sure, but two chairs like that must be worth at least a thousand pounds up in London. And oh, what beauties they were!

When the woman returned, Mr Boggis introduced himself and straight away asked if she would like to sell her chairs.

Dear me, she said. But why on earth should she want to sell her chairs?

No reason at all, except that he might be willing to give her a pretty nice price.

And how much would he give? They were definitely not for sale, but just out of curiosity, just for fun, you know, how much would he give?

Thirty-five pounds.

How much?

Thirty-five pounds.

Dear me, thirty-five pounds. Well, well, that was very interesting. She'd always thought they were valuable. They were very old. They were very comfortable too. She couldn't possibly do without them, not possibly. No, they were not for sale but thank you very much all the same.

They weren't really so very old, Mr Boggis told her, and they wouldn't be at all easy to sell, but it just happened that he had a client who rather liked that sort of thing. Maybe he could go up another two pounds – call it thirty-seven. How about that?

They bargained for half an hour, and of course in the end Mr Boggis got the chairs and agreed to pay her something less than a twentieth of their value.

From *Kiss Kiss* by Roald Dahl,
extract from *Parson's Pleasure*

1 How did Mr Boggis discover his source of supply?
   A Through nine years of driving in the country
   B By chance
   C By having a secret idea
   D By looking for it for more than nine years

2 Why did Mr Boggis walk to the farmhouse?
   A To visit his mother
   B Because he was thirsty
   C To get a new fanbelt for his car
   D To get some water for his car

3 Mr Boggis began to sweat because
   A he was afraid of something
   B it was so hot in the house
   C what he saw excited him
   D there was something on top of his head

Suggested procedure (See 1–7 on page 24)

Steps 1–4

Read the text three or more times; after doing this you should have a clear idea in your mind of exactly what has been said. You should, for example, have deduced:

what 'trade' Mr Boggis was in
It was something to do with buying and selling old furniture.

how he managed to find his source of supply
It happened by accident one day, when his car had broken down.

how he felt about the chairs
He desperately wanted them.

how he behaved with the woman
He didn't really care about her, he just wanted the chairs as cheaply as possible.

Step 5 – with Question 1

Look at the first question (*not* the answers) and try to say, in your own words, how Mr Boggis discovered his source of supply.
His car had broken down in the country and he'd gone to the nearest house to get some water; he saw the chairs there.

Step 6 – with Question 1

Look at the four possible choices, **A**, **B**, **C** and **D**, and see which of them fits best with your own answer:

A Through nine years of driving in the country
No, the nine years in the text refers to the fact that this story took place nine years before.

B By chance
Well, he presumably did not break down deliberately, and could not have known what he would find in the nearest house; so it certainly looks as though 'by chance' agrees with my own answer. (Step 5 above.)

C By having a secret idea
No, the source of supply was discovered by accident, it was not the result of any 'idea'. It is now, after the discovery, that he keeps the source secret.

D By looking for it for more than nine years
No, the discovery just happened one day, by accident.

Step 7 – with Question 1

Check that the answer you've chosen (in this case, **B**) agrees with the information given in the passage. Yes, it fits!

Now move on to the second question and repeat the procedure from Step 5 onwards.

Step 5 – with Question 2

Why did Mr Boggis walk to the farmhouse? Try to answer this question in your own words.
His car had broken down and he wanted to get some water for it.

Step 6 – with Question 2

Look at the four possible choices:

A To visit his mother
No, he was on his way home from his mother's.

B Because he was thirsty
No, he needed water for the car, not for himself.

C To get a new fanbelt for his car
This is obviously some part for the car, which he would not go to a farmhouse to get.

D To get some water for his car
Yes! This is almost exactly what I said in my own answer (Step 5).

Step 7 - with Question 2

Check your answer with what is said in the text.

Yes, it says, 'if he could please have a jug of water'.

So **D** is the right answer.

Finally, the third question:

Step 5 - with Question 3

Why did Mr Boggis begin to sweat? Think of your own answer to this.

He saw something in the farmhouse that made him very excited.

△ *Note:* If you didn't know the meaning of the word 'sweat', were you able to deduce it? There is, after all, not much than can 'come out all over the top of his head' because of excitement.

Step 6 - with Question 3

Look at the four possible choices:

A he was afraid of something
No, he was excited by something.

B it was so hot in the house
The text does not say how hot it was in the house, and although people do sweat in the heat, in this case we know that the cause of the sweat was excitement.

C what he saw excited him
Yes, the armchair.

D there was something on top of his head
No, this is silly and deliberately designed to confuse me!

Step 7 - with Question 3

Check that your choice **C** agrees with the information given in the text and answers the question.

Yes, 'he spotted something that made him so excited the sweat began to . . .'

So **C** is the right answer.

Now try to follow the same procedure for the next five questions and for the six other passages which follow.

4 The chair that interested Mr Boggis
  A was the only one of its kind
  B was supported by eight spindles
  C was carved in the form of a duck
  D was almost five hundred years old

5 Mr Boggis wanted the chairs because
  A he liked them for their beauty alone
  B they were very comfortable
  C he found them pretty and nice
  D he hoped to sell them for a profit

6 The woman thought her chairs were
  A extremely valuable
  B much less valuable than they really were
  C worth a thousand pounds in London
  D definitely not for sale

7 In the end, Mr Boggis and the woman were probably
  A satisfied that each had bargained successfully
  B dissatisfied with the bargains they had made
  C sure that the chairs would not be easy to sell
  D certain that the chairs were not really very old

8 What 'trade' was Mr Boggis probably in?
  A He made chairs
  B He was a warehouseman
  C He was a farmer
  D He bought and sold old furniture

Exercise 18

Report on new cars

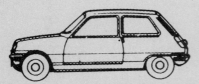

The new Hatsu Prune is certainly an improvement on the earlier Prune. It combines good reliability with a fair amount of comfort. A drawback for many people, though, will be its rather inadequate boot, not really enough for a family's luggage. More serious drawbacks are the lack of childproof locks and the underbody rust.

The Morson Mummy has, despite numerous changes during its long life, simply not kept up with the improving standards of today's cars. It has little in its favour apart from a large boot.

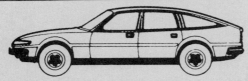

The Rigour 18 is pleasantly comfortable and adequate in most respects. But despite being the best of the bunch it is perhaps the most disappointing – as a brand-new car rather than merely a revised version, it still retains the drawbacks of earlier Rigours: heavy steering, difficult gear selection and quite a lot of body roll. (In many respects, the Rigour 18 is similar to the Rigour 12, which we've recommended as good value.) If you can tolerate its drawbacks and it proves reliable, then the Rigour 18 could make a sensible buy.

(Adapted from *Which?* Report, January 1980)

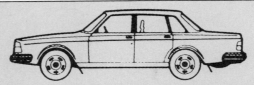

The Putomac 999, similar in size and price to the Rigour 18, is a pleasant family car with many of its strengths – all round comfort – and weaknesses – fairly heavy steering when parking, and some body roll. It's too new yet to know much about its reliability, but it looks good value.

These three cars – the Rigour 12, Rigour 18 and Putomac 999 – all offer a level of refinement better than many other family saloons. The Vixen Cavalry (and its sister the Otis Octopus), though perhaps not having quite as comfortable seats as the two Rigours and the Putomac 999, handles more crisply, without having too firm a ride. It remains our choice as the best all-rounder in this class.

1 The many changes to the Morson Mummy have
 A greatly improved its standards
 B given it a little in its favour
 C resulted in a long life
 D not really helped it to compete with other cars

2 If the one and only thing you are interested in is the amount of luggage you can carry, you might choose the
 A Putomac 999
 B Rigour 18
 C Hatsu Prune
 D Morson Mummy

3 The Vixen Cavalry is selected as generally the best because
 A of the comfort of its seats
 B of its reliability
 C of having fewer drawbacks than the others
 D of its handles

4 Which car did the testers prefer of the four below?
 A Rigour 18
 B Morson Mummy
 C Hatsu Prune
 D Putomac 999

5 Which one of the following appears to be a *good* point?
 A Heavy steering
 B Childproof locks
 C Firm ride
 D Body roll

Exercise 19

In the front desk sat George and Peter, hard at work. George was a large, stolid, slow-moving child, no match for his skinny volatile neighbour who kept up a running commentary on his actions. It was in keeping with George's (5) nature that he should have chosen to paint, with a fine brush, an elaborate scene of a village inn and a stage-coach complete with four horses in intricate harness. His paint-brush moved slowly and laboriously, his tongue (10) writhing from his mouth as he concentrated.

Beside him Peter had elected to cut out some dashing Christmas trees from gummed paper. They were done quickly he knew and would look effective. He chattered brightly to his (15) labouring companion as he folded his own first piece of green paper, and began slashing dramatically with his scissors.

'This won't take no time, George! Bet I get six done before you've half finished that old (20) thing!' The scissors flashed and triangles of green paper fell swiftly upon the desk.

'Six'll just do nicely,' continued Peter. 'Mum and Dad, and five aunties. How many do you want?' (25)

George sighed heavily.

'Ten really, but I don't expect I'll have the time.' He bent again to his task and began to paint carefully the spokes of the coach wheels. Smugly his companion opened out a beautiful (30) Christmas tree, applied a wet tongue to its back and banged it firmly down upon his folded paper.

'There!' he said triumphantly. 'One done!' George cast a morose glance upon it, but said nothing. (35)

'I might put a setting sun or a robin or something up the corner,' meditated the irrepressible Peter, head on one side. 'Got plenty of time,' he added maddeningly.

He counted five pieces of green paper, (40) stacked them together, and folded them over busily, thumping joyously with a small grubby fist. George began to outline the harness. The bells were going to be an uncommonly tricky manoeuvre. (45)

'This way,' exulted Peter, 'I can cut the whole lot out at once. Won't be no time at all. Here, you'd best get a move on with all that lot to do. Bet you don't get one finished this lesson.'

George remained silent, but by the tightening (50) of his lips Anna could see that this goading was almost more than he could bear. Had he been working alone his slow-growing masterpiece would have delighted him, but the boasting mass-producer at his side wrecked all his own (55) pleasures of creation. He plied his careful brush diligently but sadly.

Beside him Peter gave a sudden yelp of dismay. In each hand he held the fringed remnants of five decimated Christmas trees, and (60) his face was growing slowly scarlet.

'Look at that now!' said the mass-producer, vexed, 'I've been and cut through the fold!'

A smile of infinite satisfaction spread slowly across George's countenance. With a happy sigh (65) he raised his brush and set briskly to work upon the horses' tails.

From *Fresh From the Country* by 'Miss Read'

1. George and Peter
   A were working together to make a Christmas card
   B were making Christmas cards, separately
   C were sitting working silently
   D were both painting in the front desk

2. George's cards
   A were more detailed than Peter's
   B were less detailed than Peter's
   C were the same as Peter's
   D were easier to make than Peter's

3. Peter's comments on his own work and George's
   A gave George a lot of pleasure
   B helped George do a better job of work
   C took the pleasure out of George's work
   D made George so angry he couldn't control himself

4. Peter's way of working
   A was more careful than George's
   B resulted in his making a mistake
   C was very successful
   D meant that he produced six cards before George had produced his first

5. In the end George worked more successfully because he
   A had five aunties
   B used a mass-production technique
   C did his work thoroughly
   D was very clever with his scissors

Exercise 20

Our Gas Fire Safety Check will cost you £5. And it could save your life.

If your gas, wood or coal fire isn't properly ventilated and flued, it could kill you. Because a blocked chimney or flue can cause the fire to produce dangerous fumes containing a deadly, poisonous gas—carbon monoxide.

This can happen even if the fire looks to be working perfectly well—and it can happen to you!

Chimneys can deteriorate, and loose material—brickwork, mortar and old soot—can fall to the bottom, piling up on any rubble which is there already. This can quickly block the small opening that carries the fumes from your fire safely up the chimney—particularly in older homes.

WHAT TO DO

If you have a gas fire, it's easy to make sure it's safe. Call the gas people and ask for a Gas Fire Safety Check; we'll send round a service engineer to make sure that your flue is clearing the burnt fumes safely. Because we think this is so important, our Gas Fire Safety Check is subsidised—so it costs only £5 for peace of mind. This special price includes VAT, and also covers free advice on any further action which may be necessary—although the actual cost of such additional work is, of course, not included. If your gas fire hasn't been checked recently—or if you're in any doubt at all about its safety—don't take chances. Fill in the coupon or call the gas people (we're in your telephone book under 'GAS') and ask for a Gas Fire Safety Check. Your local Gas showroom can also arrange this for you.

BE A GOOD NEIGHBOUR
If any of your neighbours use gas, and you think they may not know about this service, do them a favour—bring this advertisement to their attention.

*This service does not apply to flueless convector heaters and wall heaters.

DON'T TAKE CHANCES—CALL IN THE GAS PEOPLE.

1 The aim of the advertisement is probably
  A to sell more gas fires
  B to announce changes in gas fires
  C to get more customers for gas
  D to make life safer for the public

2 If a gas fire is not checked, there may be danger from
  A the chimney
  B fumes
  C a fire
  D soot

3 Send the coupon
  A if your coal or wood fire isn't working properly
  B if you want to change your gas fire
  C if you're worried about your neighbour's gas fire
  D if you're worried about your gas fire

4 How much will it cost you to take any further action needed after your safety check?
  A Less than £5
  B £5
  C More than £5
  D We do not know

5 The dangerous situation they describe could also occur in the case of
  A coal fires
  B electric fires
  C chimney fires
  D flueless convector heaters

Exercise 21

An Englishman's 'accent' is the noises he makes when he pronounces English. A speaker from Suffolk will not use all the same noises as a speaker from Lancashire, and thus one is said to have a Suffolk accent and the other a Lancashire accent. The differences between two accents are largely a matter of pronunciation of individual sounds and of the 'tunes' that the speakers use. (5)

Though there are many different accents of English they are mostly used to speak the same English: that is, 'Standard English', the English in which this is written. If the first sentence of this text were read aloud by someone from Yorkshire, someone from Devon, and someone from Kent, the words would of course be the same, but the pronunciation would vary in each case. The speakers would not therefore be speaking 'dialect'. We use the word 'dialect' to describe the special words and word order which a particular brand of English uses, and we associate this with a particular locality. (10) (15) (20)

Of course, particular accents go with particular dialects; but we often hear someone described as 'speaking dialect' when what we mean is that he has an *accent* of some kind. (25)

In the sense described above, Standard English is itself a dialect. English was brought over to Britain by the Angles, Saxons and Jutes, and as they settled in different parts of the country, over a period of time their forms of English and their pronunciation of them began to vary. This is the origin of dialects; and thus it is wrong to claim, as is sometimes done, that one is 'older' than another. The dialect of south-east England, because it was in use in London and the court, and because books began to be written in it, became accepted as 'standard'. Accent, however, was not standard. We know that Sir Walter Raleigh kept his (30) (35) (40) Devonshire accent at the court of Elizabeth I.

From Raleigh's time the *accent* of the south-east gained greater prestige because of its associations with the capital, the court, the old universities and the public schools. It became a class accent – that of an educated ruling class. More recently, the BBC added to the status of this accent by choosing it as the one for news bulletins and announcements on official occasions. It is now known as Received Pronunciation, commonly abbreviated to 'RP'. To some people it seems the only 'correct' pronunciation of English. They even call other pronunciations 'lazy' or 'slovenly' as though there were some moral disgrace in not using Received Pronunciation. How absurd this attitude is can be seen when we consider not only the history of other accents in this country, but also the status of English as a world language. An American New England pronunciation is in no sense 'inferior' to RP, and one would not find the American who thought it was. In fact, many Americans are as irritated by RP as some English are by what they call the Americans' 'drawl'. This English attitude to accent is a matter of amazement to many overseas peoples who find nothing like it in their own countries. Of course, there must be some standards of pronunciation, otherwise we would not understand one another. The purpose of speech is after all to *communicate*. If an accent is so broad that it makes understanding difficult, then the speaker is at a disadvantage when talking to people from elsewhere. This does not mean that everyone should have the same accent, but that accents should be sufficiently alike to be mutually intelligible. (45) (50) (55) (60) (65) (70) (75)

Adapted from *In Your Own Words*
by Andrew Wilkinson

1 How do 'accents' differ from each other?
   A In the amount of noise speakers make
   B In the words that speakers use
   C In the way that people say words
   D In the special words and word order that speakers use

2 'Standard English' had its origin
   A in a local dialect
   B in the best English
   C in the oldest, 'original' English
   D in Devonshire, with Sir Walter Raleigh

3 Which is the best English pronunciation?
   A That of the educated ruling class
   B That which is spoken in the south-east
   C The one known as 'RP'
   D There is no 'best' pronunciation of English

4 Accents are a bad thing only if
   A they are used when talking to people from elsewhere
   B they are used to communicate
   C people do not have the same accent
   D they cannot easily be understood

Exercise 22

As time went on Lady Gibbons was getting more and more morose. I think by the things she let drop that money was rather tight, and that Sir Walter had made some rather unfortunate investments. Perhaps that was why (5) she was so mean, that there really wasn't very much money.

When Christmas came round I had to cook a turkey and I made a very sad job of it. I couldn't get on with that kitchen range, either I (10) made it too hot, or it wasn't hot enough. This time it was too hot and the turkey got burnt. I scraped it all off as much as I could with the nutmeg grater, I put brown breadcrumbs over the worst of the burns. I hoped for the best and (15) I sent it upstairs. I expected to hear an explosion of rage from Sir Walter, through the service lift. But all was quiet. When Olive came down I said, 'Didn't he say anything?' 'Not a thing,' Olive replied. 'What about her?' I said. (20) Olive said, 'Well, her face changed colour a bit, she turned it around, and she looked at it from all angles, but nothing was said, not from any of them.' So when two or three days had gone by and Lady Gibbons had still said nothing, I (25) began to think that perhaps it had been all right.

But on the fourth morning, out of the blue, old Lady Gibbons said to me, 'Cook, whatever happened to the turkey?' I said, 'Turkey, (30) M'Lady?' She said, 'Yes, turkey.' So I said, 'Well, it did get a bit burned.' So she said, 'A bit burned! It was just like a cinder, and when Sir Walter went to cut it, the flesh just fell off.' I said, 'Well, that's a sign of it being tender.' 'It (35) wasn't a sign of it being tender with your turkey,' she said. 'It's a pity we're not all vegetarians, because that's the only thing you can cook.' So I said, 'Well, your Ladyship, that brings me to a matter I wanted to speak to you (40) about.' I noticed she went pale at this – she thought I was going to give in my notice and that most obviously wouldn't have suited her. Burnt offering was better than no burnt offering. 'It's this,' I said. 'I thought that I might (45) take a few cookery lessons in the afternoons.'

I really had thought about this and the turkey sort of sealed matters. You see it had been my biggest failure and after all turkeys do cost a lot of money. The wretched bird was on my (50) conscience. 'That's a very good idea,' she said, her face relaxing and the colour coming back into it. Then her jaw stiffened. 'But you'll have to pay for them yourself, of course.' That leopard couldn't change her spots either. (55)

From *Below Stairs* by Margaret Powell

1. The writer
   A loved cooking turkeys
   B got on the kitchen range with the turkey
   C had an unfortunate experience cooking a turkey one Christmas
   D was very sad about turkeys

2. The turkey
   A was completely covered with brown breadcrumbs
   B looked delicious when it was sent upstairs
   C was overcooked
   D was undercooked

3 The cook thought that
  A Sir Walter would be angry when he saw her turkey
  B Lady Gibbons would think the turkey was all right
  C Lady Gibbons's face would turn many different colours
  D the turkey would be all right for Sir Walter and Lady Gibbons

4 Lady Gibbons thought that the cook
  A was a vegetarian
  B could cook vegetables quite well
  C could not cook anything
  D cooked only for vegetarians

5 Lady Gibbons went pale because
  A she hoped the cook would leave the job
  B she was afraid the cook would offer her burnt food again
  C she had just noticed something about the cook
  D she was afraid the cook might leave

6 The cook wanted to take cookery lessons because
  A she wanted something to do on her free afternoons
  B she felt bad about the food she had spoilt in the past
  C she was always thinking about turkeys
  D she was conscious of being a wretched failure

7 Lady Gibbons's jaw stiffened because
  A she had spotted a leopard
  B she was determined not to pay for the cook's lessons
  C she had just eaten a burnt turkey
  D she had to pay for the cook

 Exercise 23

HOW TO GET YOUR FREE 'CLAIM TO FAME' MYSTERY QUIZ BOOK

Simply send your name and address (block capitals please) together with 8 Walkers 'Claim to Fame' Tokens and a 18p stamp for each book you require to:

WALKERS 'CLAIM TO FAME' BOOK, P.O. BOX 6, KETTERING.

Closing date for applications for 'Claim to Fame' Books: 18th NOVEMBER 198–.
Closing date for competition entries: 16th DECEMBER 198–.
'Claim to Fame' competition entrants must be aged 16 years or over. Junior Mystery Quiz is open to children up to 16 years of age. We regret that applications not enclosing a 18p stamp will not be accepted. Please allow 21 days for delivery.

£15,000 WORTH OF PRIZES TO BE WON!

Here's your chance to enter our exciting 'Claim to Fame' competition and win a glittering prize.

1st PRIZE: £5,000 worth of GOLD SOVEREIGNS
2nd PRIZE: £2,500 worth of GOLD SOVEREIGNS
3rd PRIZE: £1,000 worth of GOLD SOVEREIGNS
plus 100 Runner up prizes of a GOLD SOVEREIGN

You'll find everything you need to help you win one of these super prizes in the FREE full colour 'Claim to Fame' Mystery Quiz Book. Within its lavishly illustrated pages are concealed the identities of 10 famous people. Reveal their names by solving the clues in the pictures, rhymes and puzzles and you are on your way to winning a golden prize. Look out for extra clues on special packets of Walkers Crisps.

1. This information was probably written in or on
   A an advertisement
   B a packet
   C a newspaper
   D a book

2. You cannot enter the Claim to Fame competition unless
   A you are over sixteen years of age
   B you are under sixteen years of age
   C you get at least one Claim to Fame book
   D you fail to send an 18p stamp for each book

3. You will have no chance of winning the first prize if you
   A send eight Walkers' Claim to Fame tokens
   B do not send in your entry for the competition before November 18th
   C send in the Claim to Fame booklet
   D do not send a stamp

4. What happens after you have got your Claim to Fame book?
   A You will win a glittering prize if you enter the competition
   B You cannot win a glittering prize unless you solve the clues
   C You will win a prize if you solve the clues
   D You will definitely win a prize if you reveal the identities of the famous people

5. The clues that you need to have a chance of winning
   A are among the pictures and words in the book
   B are printed on the crisp packets
   C are concealed in the identities of ten famous people
   D are on the Claim to Fame tokens

PAPER 2
Composition

INTRODUCTION

The regulations for the Cambridge First Certificate Examination say that students must write two compositions from a choice of topics.

This section of the book is subdivided to cover the following types of composition:

		page
1	Telling a story	37
2	Descriptions of people	44
3	Descriptions of places	49
4	Giving directions	52
5	Descriptions of objects	53
6	Prescribed texts	55
7	Letters to a friend	59
8	Semi-formal letters	63
9	Discursive writing	66
10	A talk or speech	70
11	Final notes on composition titles	72

Compositions at First Certificate level should show:

- variety and appropriateness of vocabulary and sentence structure
- correctness of grammatical construction, punctuation and spelling
- relevance to the question, and satisfactory organisation of material.

Each of the following ten sections contains at least one sample composition illustrating the various kinds of language you should try to include in your own compositions. Each sample composition is of the length required in the examination (120–180 words), and contains the sort of vocabulary and structure which can be produced by a good First Certificate candidate. The work in each section practises the vocabulary and structure illustrated in the sample, together with further practice of the language needed for each type of composition.

1 Telling a story

The following pages show how the ideas for this kind of composition are built up; they follow a pattern:

- What was the scene, when, why, where and with whom?
- What happened (and why)?
- What was the conclusion?

> **Sample question**
> Write a story which ends with the words '... one of the most exciting days of my life'.

The pattern above can be used to produce ideas for this story.

- What was the scene, when, why, where and with whom?
  Climbing a mountain; in the early morning; I'd never climbed one before; just out of a village; with some friends.

- What happened (and why)?
  Began to climb after coffee; not too difficult at first; last part joined by ropes; kept calm and reached the top; admired the view.

- What was the conclusion?
  Came down; reached the bottom as the sun was setting; day after I was stiff.

Here is a cartoon to illustrate the story, followed by a sample answer.

Sample answer

I woke at dawn and left the house quietly. My friends were waiting, and we set off from the village towards the foot of the mountain.

After stopping[1] for a quick coffee, **we began**[1] the steep walk uphill. **As**[2] this was the first time I had climbed, **I was surprised to find that**[2] it was not too difficult for me to keep going. By mid-morning, we were over half way up.

The last part of the climb was much more difficult, and if I hadn't been attached to the leader by a rope I'm sure I would have fallen: **at times**[1] I was quite frightened. **However**[2], I kept remembering the advice I had been given, not to look down, and **at last**[1] we reached the top safely. The sun was at its height, and the view was magnificent. **As**[1] the others rested, **I was so impressed that**[2] I simply stood, and stared.

We came down slowly, and **eventually**[1] reached the bottom **just as the sun was setting**[1]. **Although**[2] I was extremely stiff next day, I shall always remember my first climb as one of the most exciting days of my life.

△ *Note:* You will notice that some words and phrases are printed in **bold** type, with small figures 1 (for ways of writing about actions) or 2 (for ways of linking ideas) following them. Later we shall look at these words and phrases in more detail, and suggest how you can use them (and others) to improve your own writing. First, however, we should like you to practise planning this type of composition in the way suggested on page 37.

 Exercise 1

Remember the questions to ask yourself when writing a story:

- What was the scene, when, why, where and with whom?
- What happened (and why)?
- What was the conclusion?

Now write notes, following this pattern, about topics 1–3.

1 Describe a day when everything went wrong.
2 Tell the story of an amusing or frightening incident.
3 Give an account of a visit to a big town or to the seaside.

Ways of writing about actions

Look at these examples from the sample composition, and see how the verb tenses change in some:

a) **After stopping**[1] for a quick coffee, **we began**[1] ...
('after stopping' – first action; 'we began' – second action)
b) **at times**[1] I was quite frightened.
('at times' = sometimes)
c) and **at last**[1] we reached the top safely.
('at last' = finally)
d) **As**[1] the others rested, I ...
('as' = during the time that)
e) ... and **eventually**[1] reached the bottom **just as the sun was setting**[1].
('eventually' = finally; 'just as' = at the moment when)

Here are some other ways to introduce actions (not shown in the sample):

- *After we had reached* the top, *we sat* and ...
- *As soon as I arrived* at the church clock *we set off* ...
- *I was just about to* look down *when* I remembered the advice I'd been given.
(I didn't look down, but I nearly did)
- *While I was sitting* in the sun one of the others *was looking* for a way up.
(two actions happening at the same time)
- *It wasn't until* I started climbing *that I realised* how hard it was.
(used in dramatic situations to mean I didn't realise how difficult it was until I started climbing)
- *No sooner had I sat* down *than* our leader *set off* again.
(used in dramatic situations: 'sat down' – first action; 'set off' – second action)

 Exercise 2

Using the words in brackets, join each of the following pairs of phrases together to make a single sentence:

1 I arrived at the bus stop – at that moment the bus was leaving (*just as*)
2 paid my fare to the driver – went upstairs and sat down (*after*)
3 sat there – looked out of the window (*as*)
4 reached my stop – jumped off (*eventually*)

Exercise 3

Using the words in brackets, join each of the following pairs of sentences together to make a single sentence:

1 I almost stepped outside the front door. At that moment the fireworks exploded. (*just about to ... when*)

   [handwritten: was just about to step outside the front door when the fireworks exploded]

2 I went outside. Then I realised how much damage had been caused to the flowers. (*it wasn't until ... that*)

   [handwritten: it wasn't until I went outside that I realised]

3 I saw the damaged flowers. I burst out crying. (*as soon as*)

   [handwritten: As soon as]

4 I was looking at the damage. My cat was sleeping under a rose bush. (*while*)

   [handwritten: While]

5 I cleared up the mess. Then another lot of fireworks exploded. (*no sooner*)

   [handwritten: No sooner had I cleared up the mess than another lot of]

Exercise 4

Complete the following sentences in your own words:

1 The sea was quite rough and at times I _____.
2 She understood the problem as soon as _____.
3 We went down to the beach after _____.
4 He fell asleep just as _____.
5 The bears were sleeping in their cage while _____.

Ways of linking ideas

a) **I was surprised to find that**[2] it was not too difficult for me to keep going.

   This sentence (or a variation of it) can be used in most story-telling situations:

I was	disappointed	to	learn	that
	horrified		realise	
	surprised		see	
	delighted		find	
	amazed		discover	
	furious		hear	

   The same ideas can be expressed in the following way:

I	found	to my	surprise	that
	realised		disappointment	
	saw		horror	
	discovered		delight	
	heard		amazement	
	learnt		fury	

b) **As**[2] this was the first time I had climbed ...
   'As' means 'because' in this sentence.

c) **I was so impressed that**[2] I simply stood, and stared.

d) **Although**[2] I was extremely stiff next day, I shall always ...
   'Although' is used to join a positive idea to a negative one (or vice versa). It is put in front of the less important or subsidiary phrase. For example:

   I was extremely stiff. (negative and subsidiary phrase)
   I shall always remember. (positive and main phrase)
   Although I was extremely stiff, I shall always remember ...

   Alternatives to 'although', not shown in sample, are:

   In spite of/despite – these can be used in the same way to join positive and negative ideas together:

   He decided to go for a sailing holiday *in spite of* the fact that he was usually seasick. (or '*despite* the fact that ...')
   Despite the death of most of the animals, the zoo director decided to open as usual. (or '*in spite* of the death of ...')

e) **However**[2], I kept remembering the advice ...
   'However' is used at the beginning of the final sentence of a dramatic incident and means 'but'. Here is another example:

   I got off the train after a twelve-hour journey and was looking forward to a nice hot bath and a cup of tea in the Grand Hotel. **However**, I was disappointed to discover that there were no vacancies.

Exercise 5

Use 'I was surprised to find that...' and 'I found to my surprise that...' (or their variations) to expand the following ideas into realistic situations. Use your imagination!

Example:
A new car was standing in the drive.

a) As I opened the front door to welcome my wife home, I saw to my surprise that a new car was standing behind her in the drive. *or*
b) As I walked out of the house expecting to see my husband get out of our battered old car, I was amazed to see a new car standing in the drive, with him sitting in the driving seat.

Now do the same with these sentences:

1 Henry was playing with matches.
2 I saw the very rare bird that lives only in this area.
3 Someone dug up all the plants in my garden during the night.
4 Something dark and shapeless was standing in the corner of my bedroom.

Exercise 6

Use 'as' meaning 'because' to join each pair of sentences together:

1 I went to bed early. I was tired.
2 The weather forecast said snow. I stayed in.

Now write two sentences of your own, using 'as' in this way.

Exercise 7

Using 'so...that', join each of the following pairs of sentences together to make a single sentence, changing as few words as possible. (More practice on this and 'such...that' is given in the 'Use of English' section, page 100.)

Example:
She was extremely lively and attractive. Everyone loved her.
She was *so* lively and attractive *that* everyone loved her.

1 The weather was very bad. We couldn't climb to the top.
2 The train arrived late. We missed our appointment in London.
3 The footballer was very skilful. At times no defence was able to stop him scoring.
4 He wasn't a brilliant student but he worked very hard. He passed the exam.

Exercise 8

Use 'although', 'in spite of/despite' and 'however' with each of the pairs of sentences below. Think carefully about which of the two short sentences comes first in your answer, and which comes second: in some cases they can come in either position.

Example:
She washed her jeans twice. They still wouldn't come clean.

a) *Although* she washed her jeans twice, they still wouldn't come clean.
   or
   Her jeans still wouldn't come clean, *although* she washed them twice.
b) *In spite of* the fact that she washed her jeans twice, they still wouldn't come clean.
   or
   Her jeans still wouldn't come clean, *in spite of* the fact that she washed them twice.
c) She washed her jeans twice. *However*, they still wouldn't come clean.

1 It was raining. I went for a walk.
2 My father doesn't understand pop music. He listens to it with me.
3 She was tired. She watched TV until the closedown.
4 The fox sat and waited for hours. The rabbit didn't appear.
5 The sea was very rough. The fishermen went out in their boats.

COMPOSITION

Exercise 9

Continue the following sentences in your own words:

1 They insisted on buying me a drink although _____.

2 In spite of _____ she decided to buy the dress.

3 She really needs to get a new job; however, _____.

4 He lived to be a hundred years old despite _____.

5 Although _____, he never bought her any flowers.

6 Romeo and Juliet came from rival families; they were forbidden to meet. However, _____.

Verb tenses and forms

When you write a composition which tells a story, try to use a variety of verb tenses.

Look at these examples from the story (page 38):

a) My friends **were waiting**, and we **set off** ...
   [past continuous] [simple past]

b) As this was the first time **I had climbed**, I was
   [past perfect]
   surprised to find ...
   [infinitive]

c) **I kept remembering** the advice **I had been given**,
   [gerund] [past perfect passive]
   not to look down.
   [indirect speech]

d) ... **it was not too difficult for me to** keep going.
   [infinitive construction]

e) **If I hadn't been attached to the leader by a rope I'm sure I would have fallen.**
   [a conditional sentence including a passive construction]

Some of these tense changes have been practised on pages 38–9.

Whenever you write a composition read through the story, looking at the constructions you have used:

- How many of the tenses and constructions above have you included?
- Is your story just a series of simple past tense verbs?
- If so, can you change some of them to give your English more variety?

Exercise 10

Complete the story in the first person ('I') using the phrases given:

having	opened the door
	stepped outside
to my horror	saw a bear looking in the chicken house
so ... that	I/angry/began to shout
just as	I began to run towards him/bear turned round
as soon as	I saw this/ran back inside
it wasn't until	closed the door/realised how stupid I'd been

PAPER 2

 Exercise 11

Look back to the cartoon and the three basic questions (page 37) to remind yourself of how the ideas for a composition can be built up. Now look at the cartoon below and answer the questions, imagining you are the girl in the story:

- What was the scene, when, why, where and with whom?
- What happened (and why)?
- What was the conclusion?

Now, remember the ways of writing about actions
  (page 38)
  the ways of linking ideas (pages 39–40)
  the ways of introducing different verb tenses
  (page 41)

Write the story from a girl's point of view. The title is:
'A day when something disappointing happened'.

 Exercise 12

In an examination, composition questions which require you to tell a story may be introduced by words such as 'Write a report' or 'Describe'.

Examples:
You witnessed a road accident. Write a report for the police.

Describe the opening of a new sports stadium in your town for the local newspaper.

These questions require you to say what happened, what you saw and what you did. In other words – tell the story. (See page 72 for more examples of confusing composition titles.)

Look at the two cartoons on page 43. Tell the stories, in each case building up your composition as you did in Exercise 11.

COMPOSITION

1 You witnessed a road accident. Write a report for the police.

2 You are Rodney Smith and you work in a bank. Write a report for your local newspaper on a robbery that took place yesterday in your bank.

2 Descriptions of people

Key structures

Here are some structures to use when describing a person:
- *She is* an elderly woman.
- *Her hands are* gnarled now.
- *She has* a gentle, kind face.
- She is in her mid-seventies, *with* greying hair.
- ... always *wears* clothes that she makes herself.

A description of a person may include:
- physical description
- character description/general impressions
- something about his/her habits
- comparisons (e.g. between one member of the family and another)
- identification (e.g. how this person can be identified in a group)

Physical descriptions

Below is a small selection of words and phrases which can be used in conjunction with the key structures above to build up descriptions of people.

Study the examples carefully to see which of the key structures are used with the different words and phrases, and be particularly careful, when adding words of your own, to put them with the correct structures.

- **Age** (with the verb 'to be')
  twenty-one   a young sixty-five
  fifty years old   old; elderly; middle-aged;
                     youngish
  in her thirties   in her mid-sixties

  Examples:
  She is fifty years old.
  He was an elderly man in his mid-sixties.

- **Hair**
  colour – dark; fair; blonde; greying
  length and style – short, curly hair; long, straight hair; balding; bald

  Examples:
  He had short, fair hair.
  His hair is dark and curly.
  He is balding.

- **Eyes**
  colour – blue; brown; green
  shape – large; almond-shaped; round
  character – direct; laughing; warm; cold

  Examples:
  She has large brown eyes.
  His eyes are warm and laughing.

- **Face**
  smooth; lined; wrinkled round the eyes
  round; thin

  Examples:
  He had a round, smooth face.
  His face was lined.

- **Other facial features**
  eyebrows – bushy
  nose – turned-up
  mouth – wide; mean; generous

  Examples:
  He had bushy eyebrows and a turned-up nose.
  Her mouth was wide and generous.

- **Size and shape** (with the verb 'to be')
  big; small
  thin; slim; plump; fat
  tall; short
  broad-shouldered; well-built

  Examples:
  She was tall and thin.
  He is well-built.

- **Voice**
  deep; soft; loud; piercing

  Examples:
  Her voice was loud and piercing.
  She had a deep voice.

- **Clothes**
  an apron; a cap; a suit
  clothes that she makes herself; well-dressed
  fashionable/shabby/shapeless clothes

  Examples:
  She wears shapeless clothes that she makes herself.
  Her clothes are always fashionable.
  He was a well-dressed man.
  I was wearing my best suit.

Exercise 13

Look at the photographs on page 46 and write a physical description of each one using the key structures. You can use some of the above vocabulary together with your own.

Picture 1: My Uncle George was a very keen gardener...

Picture 2: When I arrived I saw Mrs Bloggs standing at her front door. She...

Picture 3: Wendy is...
Rodney is...

Character description/general impressions

- She *is* decisive/friendly/understanding/strict.
- She *is a* kind-hearted } sort of person.
  an easy-going
- She *has* a bad temper sometimes.
- She *seems*
  looks } happy/contented/worried.
  appears
- She always *looks* } as if she is going to laugh.
  seems
- She *looks like a* housewife.

Exercise 14

Look at the pictures on page 46 again. Write two or three sentences using the structures above about your general impression of the people and of their characters.

Habits

- She *has always loved* cooking and housework. (a life-time habit)
- Most of the time *she stays* at home. (present habit)
- When I lived at home I *always cooked* breakfast for my family. (past habit)
- I *used to* wake up much earlier. (past habit)

Exercise 15

1. Think of someone that you know and say what life-time habits he/she has had.

Use the following verbs to make your own sentences:

lived   hated   loved
worked   disliked   felt
liked   wanted   enjoyed

Example:
She *has always loved* cooking and housework.

2. Write about the regular habits of one or more of the following, using the words 'always', 'often', 'usually', 'sometimes'.

a politician   a farmer   an elephant in the zoo
a robot   your boss   yourself

Example:
He *always* has lunch with his secretary on Mondays.

3. Write five sentences describing things which you *used to do* regularly but which you *don't do now*.

Example:
When I was little I *used to* go to her with my problems.
When I was little I *always went* to her with my problems.

Comparisons

Comparing one person with another:
- She *looks like* her father. (We can see the similarity)
- She *takes after* her father. (Looks like him or is similar in character)
- My mother *is not as sympathetic as* my father.
- My present teacher *is very different from* my first one.
- My sister and I *are similar in some ways*; for instance we both like music.
- But *we differ in that* she prefers staying at home and I'd rather go out.
- My present husband is *much more handsome than* the previous one!

Comparing now with before:
- She *used to live* in London, but *now she lives* on a Scottish island.
- She *used to be* over-weight, but *not now*.

Exercise 16

Using the structures above, compare *either*: two people in your family; *or* yourself and your next-door neighbour; *or* two teachers from your school.

PAPER 2

1

cord jeans.

2

slight - over weight

3

Identification

You are sometimes asked to describe a scene in which several people are involved. Look at the photograph below and the ways of identifying the different people:

- The *woman wearing* a scarf is older than the one at the front.
- The *man with* the beard is wearing glasses.
- There's a girl at the front *who* looks young enough to be the daughter of the man with the beard.

Exercise 17

1 Look at the group photograph below and identify some of the people, using the constructions above.

2 Think of a group of people, for example:

 people at a football match
 people in a doctor's waiting room
 people at a bus stop

 and identify them using the identifying constructions.

Additional phrases

- *It wasn't* her physical appearance *that was striking but* her obvious enjoyment of life.
- When you see her *you are immediately struck* by her direct eyes.
- *Her most striking feature is* her hair which falls down to her waist.
- *You can tell* she has laughed a lot *from* the wrinkles around her eyes.

 Exercise 18

Look back at all the photographs and try to use the above additional phrases to describe some of the people. Finally, look at how some of these words and phrases have been used to answer the sample question opposite.

The photograph below is of the 'grandmother' described in the sample answer.

Sample question
Describe someone you like very much.

Sample answer
My grandmother has always been my favourite person. She is an elderly woman in her mid-seventies, with greying hair, who always wears clothes that she makes herself. You can tell that she has smiled a lot in her life from the wrinkles around her eyes. When I was young she used to live quite near our home, but since grandfather's death, she has lived with us.

She has a gentle, kind face, but when you first meet her you are immediately struck by the shrewdness of her grey eyes behind her spectacles. If ever I had a problem when I was little, I used to go to her; I knew she would understand, and be sympathetic.

She has always loved cooking and housework and still helps my mother in the house. You seldom see her without an apron round her waist. Her hands are gnarled now, and she walks with a stick, but I think she must have been very attractive when she was young. People say I take after her – I certainly hope so!

 Exercise 19

Write a description of *one* of the following people in 120–180 words, using as many as possible of the words, phrases and structures that you have practised in this section:

1. A member of your family
2. Your teacher
3. Someone you see regularly, whose appearance interests you
4. Your best friend

3 Descriptions of places

A description of a particular room, building or place could include:

- some factual information
- some impressions
- some 'human interest'

Here are some phrases that can help you to build up a description of a place:

Factual information

- **Position** – where *is* this place you are describing?
  on the left; on the ground floor; at the back of the building; overlooking the park
  opposite; between; next to; not far from, etc.
  on the coast; in the country; surrounded by forests
  40 kms from . . . ; situated in the west of the country; south of the capital; in the eastern part of the country

  Examples:
  The kitchen is at the back of the house overlooking the garden.
  Prutown is situated on the south coast of Puritania, about twenty kilometres from the regional capital.

- **Size**
  small; relatively large; tiny; average-sized
  it has a population of; it has *x* inhabitants; *x* people work there

  Examples:
  The factory is tiny; only four people work there.
  Oxford has a population of about 100,000, which is relatively small for a city.

- **General details**
  The room has (got); there are books; there is a river; it is a sleepy town with

  Examples:
  The airport has (got) three terminals with duty-free shops in each one.
  There were thousands of people trying to do their last-minute shopping before Christmas and the streets were crowded.

Exercise 20

Write down two or three sentences giving factual information about the room you are sitting in now. Think about the room's *position* in the building, its *size* and some *details* about the room itself. Look at the phrases and examples above to help you.

Exercise 21

Now do the same with your village, town or city. Give information about
1. position
2. size
3. general details.

Impressions

Here are some useful expressions for you to use when trying to give your impression of a place:

- *You are immediately struck* by the way the room is furnished. (= the first thing you notice)
- *at first sight*
- *on closer inspection*
  These two phrases are often used in the same sentence, e.g.
  At first sight the house appeared to be empty but *on closer inspection* I realised that somebody was living in one of the top floor rooms.
- *In general*, the city seems to be a place where young people can enjoy themselves.
- *The impression you get/receive* is that the university is full of life.
- *The general effect* is of an area that has been allowed to run down.
- *It looked as if* nobody had cleaned the beach for years.

Exercise 22

Write two or three sentences giving your impressions of a place to which you return after a long absence. Use some of the above phrases.

Example:
I was immediately struck by the way the city centre had changed.

The 'human interest'

If you are asked to describe a room, building, or place of any sort, try to bring in some reference to people or human activity. This will add a bit of 'life' to your composition. Think about how people are involved with the place you are describing. Here are some questions to help you think about this:

- Is anyone in the room/street/place now, and if so, what are they doing? (e.g. An old man was sitting at the pavement cafe, watching the world pass by.)
- Is there a typical human activity or feeling associated with the place? (e.g. There are often children playing in the street.)
- If there is nobody around, is there any evidence of previous human activity? (e.g. Books and papers were piled high on the desk and the floor was covered with photographs and old maps.)

Exercise 23

Look out of the window and try to describe what you see. Write your ideas down under the following headings:

Facts: (a) position (b) size (c) general details
Impressions: look back to the previous page to remind yourself of some useful phrases
'Human interest': remember to ask yourself questions like the ones shown on this page.

Exercise 24

Look at the photographs below, and write down some information about the house of your friend Suzanne. (You can see Suzanne in the kitchen.) Write down under each heading in turn: *facts, impressions, 'human interest'.*

Now look at how facts, impressions and 'human interest' are put together in the following composition:

Sample question
Write a description of a room that you enjoy being in.

Sample answer
The door on the left of the hall leads into the sitting-room, which runs the full depth of the house. As you enter, you are immediately struck by the fine view across the garden to the hills in the distance. It is a large, cheerful room with french windows leading out on to a terrace, and to the right of the main door is an attractive stone fireplace.

The furniture is old and elegant, the carpeting and decoration luxurious and tasteful. Although a lot of money has been spent, the general effect is of a room which is lived in, not just kept for visitors. In fact it is usually fairly untidy, with books, papers and teacups left lying on the chairs or tables, and the grandchildren's toys scattered around the floor.

On a winter evening, with the curtains drawn, the fire burning, and the family sitting round the card-table, it is the most welcoming place you can imagine.

Exercise 25

Study these house details and ground-floor plan (below). Write two or three paragraphs describing the house to someone who has not seen it.

```
              HOUSE DETAILS

GROUND FLOOR
Hall:           Big cupboard with water-tank; central
                heating radiator.
Sitting-room:   Good bay window; C.H. radiator;
                fireplace with all-night burner;
                good size.
Dining-room:    Large; impressive view; French
                windows to conservatory; fireplace
                with heater for hot water and C.H.
Kitchen:        Walk-in food store; stainless steel
                sink with cupboards under; lots of
                electric power points.
Conservatory:   Faces south; big; fantastic views;
                separate W.C.; walk-in store cupboard.

FIRST FLOOR
Bedrooms:       Three (similar in size and shape to
                three main downstairs rooms).
Bathroom:       With C.H. radiator.
W.C.            Separate.

OUTSIDE
Drive-way:      Plenty of room for cars.
Sheds:          Two.
Garden:         Back and front (back - good size).
```

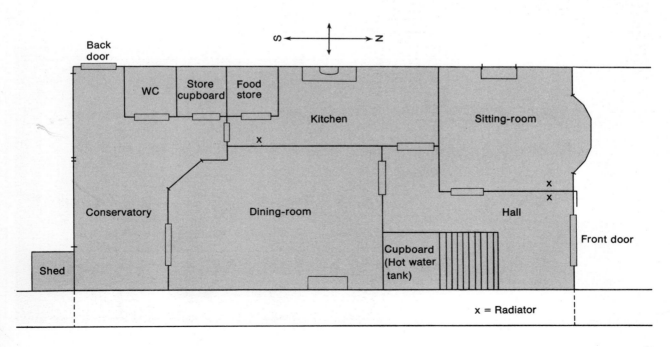

PAPER 2

where, how, when

4 Giving directions

It is possible that you may have to write street directions in answer to an examination question, either as part of a composition or as a guided writing exercise in Paper 3. Below is an example of how to write down directions:

Go along Leyland Road past the football ground until you come to Forest Way. Turn left into Forest Way and keep straight on through the first set of traffic lights and over the river for about half a kilometre, until you come to a big roundabout. You can either keep straight on into Station Road, or it might be better to go off to the right along King's Road. Once you're in King's Road, take the second turning on the left – don't go down the first street, that only goes to the car park. Turn left at the traffic lights, go along to the end of Eastern Avenue, and you'll find yourself in the High Street. Turn right, and when you get to the end of the High Street you'll see the bus station on your left, opposite the main Post Office. Go round the corner to the left into Pembroke Drive, and if you keep going for about two hundred metres you'll see it on your right. It shouldn't take you more than about five minutes by car.

Exercise 26

When you have read and understood the passage, go through it again and see if you can fill in, on the map below, the names of the streets and buildings that are mentioned. Start from the point marked 'X'. You can check your answers by looking at the complete map in Test Paper 3, page 167.

Exercise 27

Look again at the passage and notice the words and phrases which have been used to give directions.

Examples:
Go along . . . past . . . until you come to . . .
Turn left into . . . keep straight on . . .

Pick out more examples and then practise using them by writing down in a short paragraph the directions you would give to a stranger in your own town (for example, from the train or bus station to a bank).

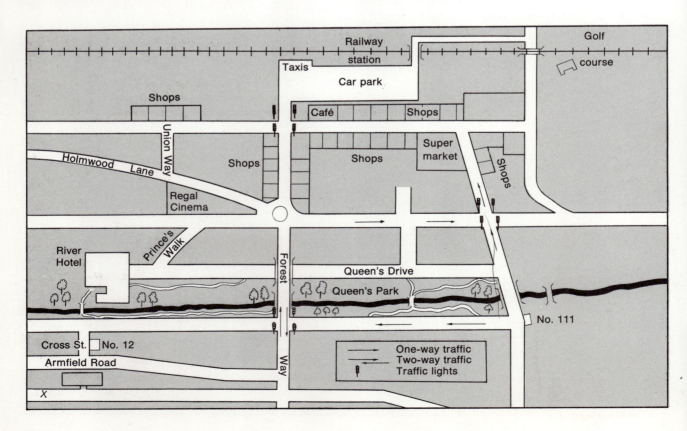

It's small, round, flat, gold with a brown crocodile leather strap. dark- tall, hand, Roman Numerals winder.

5 Descriptions of objects

It is unlikely that you will be asked to write 120–180 words describing a single object, but quite possible that you may have to describe something as *part* of a composition (look at the sample on page 54). Here are some headings to help you organise such a description:

- **Purpose**
  People use it to . . . (e.g. open bottles).
  It is used to . . . (e.g. open bottles).
  You can (e.g. open bottles) with this.
  It is for (e.g. opening bottles).

- **Size**
  big, small; long, short
  It is (2 m) long/wide/high/in diameter/in length.
  From one end to the other it is about (2 m)

- **Shape**
  It is thin/broad/flat.
  It is round   square   triangular

  It is   oval (in shape) ✓

  It is tubular   rectangular ✓

  spherical   irregular (in shape)

  It is a   square-shaped object.

It is straight   curved

a silver and gold bracelet

pointed   jagged.

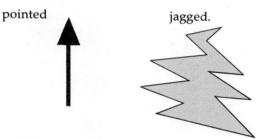

It is shaped like a . . . (e.g. pear).

- **Texture or quality**
  It is hard/soft/smooth/rough/blunt/sharp.

- **Appearance**
  It is shiny/dull-looking.
  It is light blue/dark blue/greyish/grey-green/multi-coloured.
  It is patterned/striped/plain.

- **Made of**
  It is made of wood/plastic/metal.
  It is made of some sort of man-made material.

- **Weight**
  It is hollow/solid/light/heavy.
  It weighs a lot/very little.
  It's too heavy to lift.

- **Additional details**
  At one end there is . . .
  At the other (opposite) end there is . . .
  At both ends there are . . .
  At the top end/thick end/thin end there is/are . . .
  On one side there is . . .
  On the other (opposite) side there is . . .
  On both sides there are . . .
  At each corner (of the table) there are . . .
  On top . . .
  Underneath . . .

- **How it is used**
  Push it into the cork *by turning* until it has appeared through the other side. *Then, holding* the bottle firmly with one hand, *pull* the corkscrew with the other and the cork *will* come out.

a fairly large, light heavy -brown, irregular Rectangler shaped, tough wooden, hand-made table with graffiti

Exercise 28

Look at these photographs. Following the headings on this and the previous page (Purpose, Size, Shape, etc.) describe the objects. It is not always possible to use all the headings for each object.

Now look at how these details are put together in a sample composition. The first paragraph contains no description of the object; it is concerned with 'setting the scene'.

Sample question
You have been asked to write a statement for the police describing your watch, which has been stolen. Include in your statement the circumstances surrounding its disappearance.

Sample answer
I remember taking my watch off early on Saturday evening to have a shower, and putting it on the table next to my bed. In the middle of the concert at the Festival Hall that night I noticed I hadn't got my watch on. When I got home, I went straight to my bedroom to pick it up and found that the window was broken and the watch had gone. Nothing else had been taken as far as I know.

The watch was gold and had a round face. It was slim and had hands – not one of those digital ones. There were little marks, like lines, on the face to mark the hours instead of numbers and it had a small knob at the side to wind the watch. It was made in Switzerland but I can't remember the make.

On the back of the watch there was a small star-like engraving, which I put on all my precious things as a way of identifying them. The strap was made of black leather, and had a gold fastening.

6 Prescribed texts

Question number 5 in the composition section of the examination is based on three 'prescribed texts'. One question will be set on each of the three books and you may, if you wish, answer *one* of these three questions. You are not obliged to write a 'prescribed texts' answer, and you are, therefore, not obliged to read any of the books. (It is not possible, of course, to answer a 'prescribed texts' question if you have not read the relevant book.)

However, there is nothing particularly difficult or frightening about attempting this question. The kind of writing you have to do is similar to that practised on pages 37–51, *Telling a story* and *Description*. Reading the books can help to widen your knowledge of vocabulary and could well be an enjoyable experience. It also means that you can go into the examination knowing you have a possible choice of five questions, rather than only four if you have not prepared yourself for the 'prescribed texts' questions.

It is advisable to read all three set books, or at least two. If you read only one, and the question you are asked to answer is not a 'friendly' one, then you have wasted your preparation time. Reading two or three books, particularly with the sort of thorough and systematic approach described below, will take you a long time. It is no use beginning to prepare if you do not have the time and patience to see it through to the end. It is also no use preparing if you do not enjoy reading.

If you have decided to attempt the 'prescribed texts' question, the following pages will help you to prepare for the examination.

Suggested procedure

1. Read right through the book. Underline those words which are unfamiliar to you, look them up in your bilingual dictionary, and pencil in the translation over the underlined English word. Doing this will take some time, but it is the basis for all the rest of your work on the book.

2. Read the whole book again, this time for enjoyment! At the same time you will get a much clearer general 'overview' of the story.

3. Go through the book again, this time *taking notes* under specific headings (e.g. characters, places, events, etc.). You should reserve a separate page in your notebook for each heading, and write down *anything* which adds to your knowledge of the person, thing, place, etc. Here are some suggested headings:

   - Characters in the story
   - Places
   - Events
   - Institutions, organisations etc
   - Things
   - Relationships
   - Any other points specific to the book

   The headings will, of course, vary according to the book you are studying. On page 57 you will find some examples of headings and notes taken on one specific book.

4. Write some practice compositions on the set text: see page 58 for some ideas.

5. Read the whole book a last time, preferably some time *after* completing stage 3, and not too long before the examination.

We shall illustrate the 'suggested procedure' with examples from one particular book, *The Hound of the Baskervilles*, by Sir Arthur Conan Doyle. This is the kind of book likely to be set as a prescribed text; of course you have probably not read it, but if you read the summary on page 56, you should have a clear enough idea of the people and events in the book to understand the examples of notes you might make, and compositions you might have to write, which follow.

Summary

Sherlock Holmes and Dr Watson are asked by Dr Mortimer to investigate the suspicious death of his old friend Sir Charles Baskerville, owner of Baskerville Hall, and the legend of an evil hound which is said to have caused the death of many of the Baskervilles. Watson goes to Baskerville Hall, which is situated in the middle of wild and desolate Dartmoor, with the new owner, Sir Henry Baskerville. On their arrival, they find out that a dangerous criminal, Selden, is hiding on the moor. Later they discover that Mrs Barrymore, a servant at the Hall, is Selden's sister.

Sherlock Holmes, unknown to Watson and Sir Henry, has been hiding on the moor in order to watch people's movements without them knowing. He believes that Stapleton (a neighbour of the Baskervilles) wants to kill Sir Henry. Stapleton appears to be using two women (his wife, who is pretending to be his sister; and Laura Lyons, who loves him) to help him with his aim, although the women know nothing of his evil intentions. Selden, the escaped prisoner, is found dead on the moor after terrible howling cries have been heard: he appears to have been killed by a large wild animal, and he is wearing old clothes of Sir Henry's, which had been given to him by Mrs Barrymore. Perhaps there really is a 'hound', and perhaps someone intended it to kill the wearer of the clothes whose scent it had been trained to recognise!

Holmes and Watson make a plan to prove Stapleton's guilt. They persuade Sir Henry to accept an invitation to dinner at Stapleton's isolated house on the moor. Sir Henry leaves the Stapletons' house after dinner, and begins to cross the moor to return home. The terrifying animal cries are heard again, and a huge hound appears and attacks Sir Henry. Holmes shoots the hound and Sir Henry is saved. When they return to Stapleton's house he has disappeared, leaving his wife a prisoner to prevent her from warning people of the terrible things she now suspects about her husband.

The next morning Holmes and Watson look for Stapleton but do not find him. Instead they find evidence that he has fallen into the 'mire' (wet land in which a person can sink) during the night, and died horribly. They discover a secret hiding place in the middle of the moor, where Stapleton had obviously kept the hound. Stapleton had killed Sir Charles, and was trying to kill Sir Henry, because he was a distant relative of the Baskervilles whom nobody had known about; he would inherit Baskerville Hall and the family fortune if the other Baskervilles died.

The following are examples of the kind of headings and notes you might make on this book.

Characters

Sir Henry Baskerville
Son of Sir Charles's second brother. Small, dark-eyed, eager man. About thirty. Very strongly built. Thick black eyebrows, sunburnt. Hot tempered (like all the Baskervilles). Received £740,000 on death of Uncle Charles. Keen on Beryl Stapleton, etc.

Beryl Stapleton
Beautiful, dark proud face, dark eager eyes. Tall, slim, fashionably dressed. Warns Watson to go back to London immediately, and not stay on the moor. Seems concerned about and fond of Sir Henry. Turns out to be wife, not sister of Stapleton. Very loyal to husband, etc.

Places

The moor
Frightening – not a place to go to at night. Very few people live there. Princetown Prison for dangerous criminals is on the moor. Strange places – stone rings, which were homes of early men, and Grimpen Mire, area of wet land that sucks down people, etc.

Events

Death of Sir Charles Baskerville
Death believed to be from natural causes – he had a bad heart. Friend and doctor, Dr Mortimer, is suspicious. Sir Charles found dead by Barrymore on night of 4 June in garden. No signs of violence but ugly, twisted expression on face. Footprints of a gigantic hound found near the body, etc.

Relationships

Between Stapleton and Beryl Stapleton
Beryl was known as his sister. He was jealous of her when she showed affection to Sir Henry Baskerville. Holmes discovered she was Stapleton's wife. Very loyal to husband, loved him a lot. He tried to use her in his plans, etc.

Other

The legend of the Hound of the Baskervilles
In 1650 Baskerville Hall owned by Hugo Baskerville, a wicked man who kidnapped a young girl and imprisoned her. She escaped and in his anger Sir Hugo promised to give his body and soul to the Powers of Evil if he got her back again. He set off across the moor with his hounds, followed later by thirteen friends, etc.

Sample question A
Explain how the women in the story were caused much unhappiness by the wickedness of men.

Sample answer A
There were three women in the story who were made unhappy by men. Mrs Barrymore, the servant at Baskerville Hall, was unhappy because of her brother, Selden, who was an escaped murderer from Princetown prison. The Barrymores gave Selden shelter, and later gave him food when he was living on the moor. Mrs Barrymore was caught between being loyal to a brother, but not wanting to help a wicked criminal.

Mrs Stapleton was made unhappy by her husband. She suspected the terrible things he was planning, but kept quiet through fear. He used to beat her, but she was prepared to suffer anything for his love. When she discovered a rival in Laura Lyons, her love turned to hatred.

There were two men who caused Laura Lyons unhappiness; the first was her husband who had deserted her but still had legal powers over her, and the second was Mr Stapleton. She did not know he was married and when she discovered this she realised she had been used by him for his own evil purposes.

Sample question B
Describe the hall, its garden and the moor, and say something about how the atmosphere of the surroundings influences the story.

Sample answer B
Baskerville Hall is situated in a hollow in the middle of Dartmoor. The front of the hall is covered in ivy and this makes it appear dark and heavy. It is a very old building and does not give the feeling of being a very friendly place. Surrounding the hall, there is a large garden which opens on to the moor. It was in the part of the garden called Yew Alley that Sir Charles's body was found.

Beyond the garden is the moor, a strange and rather frightening place where mists can appear very quickly. One part of the moor, called the Mire, is a very dangerous place where a person can sink into the ground and disappear. There is a prison for dangerous criminals on the moor and this seems to add to the bad feelings that the place produces. There is only one person who seems happy on the moor and that is Stapleton, who uses the moor to help his evil intentions.

Further examples of possible questions

- Describe Sir Henry's journey from London to Baskerville Hall and the first few hours he and Dr Watson spent in the old family home.
- Write about the part played in the events of the story by Miss/Mrs Stapleton.
- 'As you value your life and your reason keep away from the moor.' Write an account of Sherlock Holmes's investigation into the mystery, from the time Sir Henry showed him this strange message to the time Dr Watson and Dr Mortimer left for Devonshire.
- Write an account of Dr Watson's first meeting with the Stapletons of Merripit House.
- In what ways was the escaped convict, Selden, involved with the other characters in the story?

Questions on other prescribed texts

Finally, here are some question 'skeletons' for you to use when preparing for *any* prescribed text. Put in the appropriate names, places, etc. to fit the book you have been reading, and then write your practice compositions.

- Describe how ... (place, building) is important in the story.
- Trace the course of events from after the ... (murder, death, disappearance, other dramatic event) until the end of the story.
- Why did ... (a character) behave as he/she did? Outline the main reasons for his/her conduct.
- Write about the part in the story played by ... (any thing, institution, organisation, etc. that is important).
- Retell the story of the ... (any particularly significant event in the story).
- Describe ... (one significant building, place or town), and then describe, by contrast, ... (a very different building, place or town).
- Who was ... (an important character, but not one of the principal ones) and what part does he play in the story?
- Write about the course of the relationship between ... and ... (two characters who have a significant relationship!)
- Write a description of the ... (a significant meeting, conference, event in the story).
- Write an account of the occasion when ... (someone in the story did something, went somewhere, experienced something, etc.).
- Give some examples of the contribution of ... and ... (anything or anybody of special significance in your book) to the course of events.
- What do we learn from this book about ... (anything specific in the subject-matter which is new, unusual or significant)?

7 Letters to a friend

Layout of the letter

- **Address**
  Your address (not your name) should be in the top right-hand corner, arranged in the following way:
  Number or name of house; street or road
  Town
  Region or county; postcode
  Country (if necessary).
- **Date**
  The date should be under the address. It can be written in different ways:
  11th October, 198–.
  October 11th, 198–.
  11/10/8– (This can be confusing, as it means different things in different countries.)
  11 October 198– (This form, with no punctuation, is frequently used in modern offices.)
- **Salutation**
  Dear Bob, (the salutation) should be against the left-hand margin and should have a comma after it.
- **Paragraph 1**
  The first paragraph traditionally begins under the first letter of the correspondent's name (in the example, the 'B' of 'Bob'). However, it is now acceptable to start the letter against the left-hand margin.
- **Endings**
  There are many ways of ending a friendly letter. Here are some: With love, With best wishes, Kind regards, Yours, All my love,
- **Signature**
  Write the signature in the middle of the page.

Exercise 29

1 Put the following in the correct positions and with the correct punctuation as they would appear at the beginning of a letter:
   Littlewood Road 22   England   198– June 14
   London WC3 3NC

2 You are asked to write a letter to a friend in England. Write the address, date, salutation and ending (with signature) for this letter. Put them in the correct positions.

Structure of the letter

a) Salutation (see *Layout*)
b) First paragraph – introduction
c) Second and third paragraphs – information that has to be communicated
d) Fourth paragraph – conclusion
e) Ending (see *Layout*)
f) Signature

Here are some useful phrases for the first and last paragraphs of a letter to a friend.

Introducing a letter, and general newsy phrases

- I'm (just) writing to { tell you (that) ... / let you know (that) ... / etc.
- I thought I would just { write / drop you a line } to ...
- Just a short note to ...
- Thank you for your letter. It was lovely to hear from you (again).
- Sorry I haven't written to you for so long. I've been very busy and I just haven't had the time.
- I've been meaning to write to you for ages, but I'm afraid I just haven't got round to it.
- It's ages since I heard from you so ...
- What a surprise hearing/seeing/getting a letter ...
- I met John the other day and he told me ...
- I've just heard that ...

Ending the letter

- Jill sends her regards.
- Regards from Jill.
- My regards to your parents.
- I hope to hear from you soon.
- I'm looking forward to { hearing from you soon / seeing you ... / your reply.
- Write soon and { tell me / let me know } { whether ... / when ... / where ...
- See you { soon / on Saturday.

PAPER 2

> **Sample question**
> Write a letter to a friend apologising for the disagreement you had, which you now consider to have been your fault, at your last meeting.

Sample answer

> 96 Union Street,
> Blackport,
> Thameside,
> TH6 9SX
>
> 29th March, 198_.
>
> Dear Bob,
>
> <u>I'm writing to</u>[1] <u>apologise for</u>[2] the disagreement we had last week. I've been thinking about it and <u>I was to blame</u>[2] — I think we did agree to meet at 7.30 p.m., and not 8.30 pm.
>
> <u>Anyway</u>[1], I would like to see you again next week. <u>Why don't we</u>[2] meet on Wednesday at 7.30 p.m. in the Red Lion and <u>then perhaps go</u>[2] to the cinema, if there's anything good on? <u>If this is no good</u>[2] for you, <u>could you</u>[2] ring me at the office and we'll arrange another day? My number is 73654, extension 22.
>
> <u>I do hope</u>[1] you'll forget our quarrel. As I said, I know it was <u>my fault</u>[2]. I had had a really hectic day at <u>the office</u>[2], and when we met I was in a bad mood. <u>That's why</u>[2] I said all those horrible things to you.
>
> <u>I'm very much looking forward to seeing</u>[1] you next week.
>
> With love,
> Jane

General phrases

The phrases that have been keyed with a figure 1 can be used in most informal letters.

a) **I'm writing to**[1]
   apologise for ...
   thank you for ...
   congratulate you on ...
   tell you that ...
   invite you to ...
   let you know that ...
   ask you if ...

b) **Anyway**[1], ...
   This is a useful word at the beginning of the second or third paragraph to introduce the main point, or to change the subject:

   Example:
   Anyway, I would like to see you again next week.

c) **I do hope**[1] you'll ...
   The reason why the word 'do' is included is to emphasise the hope. 'I hope' is expressing my wish. 'I do hope' is expressing a strong wish.

d) **I'm very much looking forward to seeing**[1] you next week.
   A good sentence with which to end a letter. Look carefully at the verb ending
   '... forward to see*ing* you ...'

Other useful phrases

The phrases in the sample which are underlined, keyed with a figure 2, express the three purposes of the letter:

a) apology
- I'm writing to **apologise** for² ...
- **I was to blame**² ...
- **It was my fault**²

b) explanation
- **I had had a really hectic day**² ...
- **That's why**² ...

c) arrangement
- **Why don't we**² meet ... ?
- and **then perhaps go**² to the cinema
- **If this is no good**² for you, **could you**² ... ?

There are many reasons for writing letters, and below is a list of phrases which can be used for particular purposes:

1 Giving good news
- You'll be delighted to hear (that) ...
- I've got some marvellous news ...

2 Replying to good news
- I was delighted to hear (that) ...
- Congratulations on passing the exam.

3 Giving bad news
- I'm afraid I've got some bad news { for you. / to tell you.
- I felt you ought to know (that) ...

4 Replying to bad news
- I was sorry to hear (that) ...

5 Thanking
- Thanks for lending me your bike.
- Thank you for your letter.
- Thank you for sending me those beautiful flowers.
- It was very kind of you to ...

6 Asking someone to do something for you
- I wonder if you could ... ?
- I wonder if you could do me a favour?
- Do you think you could ... ?

7 Agreeing to a request
- I'd be delighted to ...
- Of course I'll ...

8 Asking for permission
- Do you mind if I ... ?
- Do you think I could ... ?

9 Refusing a request
- I got your letter the other day asking ... but I'm afraid I can't help you.
- I'm afraid it's just impossible.
- You know I would help you if I could but ...

10 Inviting
- We're having a party on Saturday and we were wondering if you would be able to come.
- It'll be lovely if you can come.

11 Accepting an invitation
- I was delighted to get your invitation ... I'd love to come.
- Is it all right if I bring a friend with me?
- Is it all right if I come a bit later on?

12 Refusing an invitation
- Thank you very much for your invitation, but I'm afraid I won't be able to come.
- Perhaps we'll be able to arrange something for another time.

13 Advising/recommending/suggesting
- Why don't you/we ... ?
- Let's go ...
- If I were you, I'd ...
- I think { you should ... / we should ...

14 Giving details of plans, etc.
- I'm coming on the 8.30 train. Will you be able to meet me at the station?
- I'm thinking of going to the States for the summer.
- I plan to visit Washington.

15 Putting off an arrangement
- I'm afraid I won't be able to ... after all.

16 Apologising
- I'm writing to apologise for ... ing ...
- I'm sorry about ...
- I'm sorry { I didn't ... / I wasn't able to ...

17 Wishing someone good luck

- Good luck with your interview.
- I hope everything goes well on Friday.

 Exercise 30

Write one or two sentences for the following letters. The numbers at the end of each title refer to the information given on pages 61–2.

1. A letter thanking some English friends for having you to stay. (5)
2. A letter replying to some bad news about your exam results. Your teacher wrote and told you the results. (4) (5)
3. A letter asking a friend to let you use his/her apartment by the sea for the weekend. (6) or (8)
4. A letter from the friend (in **3** above) saying you can't use the apartment because . . . (9)
5. A letter giving advice to a friend who has a problem, and wishing her luck with it! (13) (17)
6. A letter of invitation to a party. (10)
7. A letter accepting the invitation. (11)
8. A letter refusing the invitation. (12)
9. A letter agreeing to a friend's request for you to look after her ten-year-old child for a day. (7)
10. A letter thanking your uncle who has given you a large sum of money and saying what you'll do with it. (5) (14)
11. A letter to a friend (girl or boy) telling her/him of your plans to get married and go to live in the USA. (1) (14)
12. A letter to a relative explaining why you haven't been able to visit her/him recently and what you've been doing. (16)
13. A letter to a friend who has just had twins. (2)
14. A letter to your aunt, who has been looking forward to seeing you, saying you won't be able to come and visit her after all. (3) (15)

 Exercise 31

Write a complete letter to a friend giving news of yourself and asking about her/him.

COMPOSITION

8 Semi-formal letters

Layout of the letter

- **Address**
  Your address (not your name) should be in the top right-hand corner; the address of the person to whom you are writing should be on the left-hand side.
  Look at the sample letter on the next page for the exact positions.

- **Date**
  On the right, under your address.
  (Again, look at the sample letter.)

- **Salutation**
  'Dear Sir (or Madam),' should be against the left-hand margin, with a comma after it.
  If you know the name of the person you are writing to, use it, e.g. 'Dear Mr Johnson,'.

- **Paragraph 1**
  Begin the first paragraph under the 'S' of 'Sir'.

- **Endings**
  If you begin the letter 'Dear Sir (or Madam)' you must end
      'Yours faithfully,'.
  If you begin 'Dear Mr Johnson,' you must end
      'Yours sincerely,'.

- **Signature**
  Write the signature in the middle of the page.

Structure of the letter

a) Salutation (as above)
b) First paragraph – introduction
c) Second paragraph – facts
d) Third paragraph – action
e) Fourth paragraph – conclusion
f) Signature

Here are some useful phrases for the first and last paragraphs:

General introductions
- I'm writing to enquire whether ...
- I've been recommended by Mr Potts to write to you about ...

Closing remarks
- I look forward to { hearing from you. / your reply.
- I hope to hear from you as soon as possible.

> **Sample question**
> Write a letter to the manager of a travel agency in England asking about the possibilities of your working for them.

Exercise 32

Lay out letters with the salutations and signatures from the following information. Remember to punctuate.

1 From: 123 Harrow Way   Liverpool 12
         29th December 198–

   To: Mr J Johnson   Barclays Bank plc
         122 Broad Street   Liverpool

2 From: Acme Supplies Ltd   93 Castle Street
         Manchester 2   2 August 198–

   To: The Manager   Littlefords Co Ltd
         93 Parliament Hill   Cambridge

Sample answer

atcetera

8 Curdson Way,
Sittingdown,
Muffetshire MU3 2RU

14th June, 198_.

The Manager,
Berlin Travel Agency,
124 Buckingham Road,
London WC1 8PX

Dear Sir,
    I am writing to enquire whether there is any possibility of my working for your branch in Germany as a guide to British tourists.
    As you will see from the enclosed curriculum vitae, I went to a college in Hamburg **to study** English. My course there concentrated on spoken English, and we were sent to England for three months to study part-time in language schools.
    Since I finished the course I have been working in a travel agency in Hamburg, organising tours and excursions for tourists from all over the world. **Although I enjoy this work I feel** it is time for me to broaden my experience, and I think that acting as a guide to British tourists would provide the challenge I need.
    I enclose the addresses of **my college and my present employer** who **will be glad to give you references.** As I am in England for the next month it would be convenient for me to come for an interview during this time, and I look forward very much to hearing from you.

                              Yours faithfully,

                              H. Braun

                              Heidi Braun

Types of letter

The phrases that have been printed in bold in the sample are often used in letters that give information about yourself (or someone else).

a) **As you will see from the enclosed curriculum vitae, I went to** a college in Hamburg **to study** ...
b) **Since I finished the course I have been working** ...
c) **Although I enjoy this work I feel** ...
d) **My college and my present employer will be glad to** ...

There are other reasons for writing formal or semi-formal letters. Here are some phrases which will be helpful. The letters (b), (c), (d), (e) refer to the entries shown under *Structure of the letter* on page 63.

Applying for a job/giving information/getting information

- I have seen your advertisement in today's copy of *The Times* and would like to apply for the post of General Manager. (b)

- I am enclosing a curriculum vitae, together with a reference from my last employer. (c)

- I shall be glad to supply any further information you may require. (d)

- I should be grateful if you could send me an application form. (d)

Complaining

- I have been (eating in your restaurant) regularly for ten years but I feel I must complain about the poor service I received yesterday. (b)
- I'm sorry to say that (six of the items were broken on arrival) (c)
- I have now been waiting over two months for . . . (c)
- I shall have no alternative but to cancel the order. (d)
- I should be interested to know what explanation you can give for this . . . (d)

Answering an advertisement

- I saw your advertisement in yesterday's 'Manchester Star' for (a 1986 Mini) and . . . (b)
- I am looking for . . . (c)
- Would it be possible for me to . . . ? (d)

Recommending someone or something

- This is to recommend Miss Baker as a person who . . . (b)
- I have known Miss Baker for eight years and . . . (c)
- She has always been . . . (a hard worker, etc.) (c)
- I have no hesitation in recommending her for . . . (d)

Resigning

- I am writing to let you know that I have decided to resign from the company. (b)
- I have been very happy here but . . . (c)
- I shall always remember the time I spent here. (d)
- I should like to wish you every success in the future. (e)

Exercise 33

Look at the way the sample letter follows the 'Structure of the letter' on page 63.

- introduction – reason for writing (b)
- facts – details of training (c)
- action – what are you doing now and what you want to do (d)
- conclusion – asking for an interview (e)

Follow this pattern for the four paragraphs and write notes for the following:

1 You saw an advertisement in the newspaper for holiday brochures. Write to the company telling them where you saw the advertisement, what you need, and ask them to send you information.

- introduction
- facts
- action
- conclusion

2 You bought a radio from your local department store recently and it has been unsatisfactory. Write to them to complain about this.

- introduction
- facts
- action
- conclusion

Exercise 34

Write a letter of application for a job, including a short history of your life. Say where the employer can apply for a reference. Look at this and the previous page for guidance.

Exercise 35

Write the following letters using the phrases for the different types of letters as given on the previous pages.

1 You have seen an advertisement for some chairs. Write for more information and a brochure.

2 You are a member of a club. Write to the secretary and tell him you want to resign and why.

3 Write a letter to the manager of a restaurant to complain about the poor quality of the food and the high prices.

4 Write to an English language school in England, recommended to you by a friend, to find out about courses, accommodation, cost.

5 Write to a former teacher or professor to tell him/her the progress you have made since you last saw him/her.

6 Write a letter to the manager of a company in your town, recommending an English friend of yours who has applied to work there as a translator/interpreter.

9 Discursive writing

Some composition topics require you to discuss the advantages and disadvantages of something, or to give your opinion.

Sample question A
What are the advantages and disadvantages of air travel?

Look at the notes for this composition:

Advantages (+)	*Disadvantages* (−)
Quick	No feeling of travelling
Easy	Don't see countries on the journey
Comfortable	Tired
Relatively cheap	Weather delays

Now see how these notes have been expanded into a full composition.

Sample answer A
The first obvious advantage of air travel is that it is quick. You can fly from Europe to America in a matter of hours, and with the introduction of supersonic planes, time between continents is getting shorter. It is very easy travelling by plane; someone looks after your luggage and all you have to do is get on, sit down and enjoy a meal or a film. Your comfortable seat is reserved and there is excellent waitress service. **Another point in favour of air travel is** that it is relatively cheap, especially for long-distance travel.

On the other hand, travelling by air has some disadvantages. Perhaps the most important is that you fly directly to your destination and you have no feeling of travelling from one country to another. **Another point is that** because air travel is so quick, people going long distances often suffer from tiredness; so they save time travelling, **but** waste time recovering. **One other disadvantage is** that passengers are very often delayed by fog and so the advantage of speed is cancelled.

 Exercise 36

Write down four advantages and four disadvantages for each of the following:

1 Being an only child (no brothers or sisters)
   Advantages   *Disadvantages*
2 Television
   Advantages   *Disadvantages*
3 Being a politician
   Advantages   *Disadvantages*

Sample question B
Do you think old people should be looked after by their families when they become too old to manage by themselves? If so, give your reasons; if not, say why not, and suggest how they should be looked after.

This composition requires something a little different from the first one. Here you must *give your opinion* and *give reasons* and *suggestions*. Look at the notes for this composition:

Opinion	I do not think that old people should be looked after by their families.
Reasons	difficult to be looked after properly; relationships between generations not easy.
Suggestions	financial assistance from the state; government nursing system; special homes; special housing areas with supervision.

Sample answer B
The problem of looking after old people is greater today than ever before. **It is difficult for them to** be properly cared for by the family because quite often both parents go out to work. **Another problem is** that nowadays the relationship between two generations in one house is often difficult; with three generations it may be impossible.

Bearing this in mind, I think that old people **should** be the state's responsibility, not the family's. They should be looked after financially, so that they can end their lives without worrying about money. **If** they wish to live in their own homes, but need special care, **this should come** from a government nursing system.

In many countries old people can live in special homes; public money should be spent on building more of these, and improving their facilities. Even better would be old people's flats or bungalows, grouped together and under the supervision of trained staff.

To sum up, I believe that families cannot look after their old people satisfactorily nowadays, and that this should be the responsibility of the state.

Exercise 37

Write down ideas for the following subjects. Remember, make your decision and then say *why* it is your opinion.

1 Do you think dogs should be prohibited from towns and cities? If so, say why; if not, say why not.
   Opinion
   Reasons

2 All pupils should be forced, by law, to stay at school until they are eighteen. Do you agree with this? If so, say why; if not, say why not and say what should happen.
   Opinion
   Reasons
   Suggestions

3 Dangerous sports like motor racing and boxing should be banned. Do you agree? If so, say why; if not, say why not.
   Opinion
   Reasons

> **Sample question C**
> A dog or a cat – explain which in your opinion makes a more suitable companion for an old lady.

If you think about this question for a moment you will see that it is much more complicated than the first two types in this section: sample question A compared the advantages and disadvantages of one subject (air travel), whereas now you have to take into account first the good and bad points of cats, then the good and bad points of dogs, before deciding which, on balance, is the 'winner'.

It is obviously important to organise one's thoughts clearly; the tables below show how, in this case, the various negative and positive points about the two animals might be arranged.

Setting things out in this way can help you to avoid confusion.

Cats	
Good points (+)	**Bad points (−)**
cheap	too independent
easy to keep	not as loving
look after themselves	catch birds
nice to hold and stroke	

Dogs	
Good points (+)	**Bad points (−)**
give pleasure	expensive
companionship	need exercise
make friends	
guard	

> **Sample answer C**
> An old lady's choice of pet will depend on her circumstances – whether she lives alone, what kind of house or neighbourhood she lives in, and whether she is rich or poor.
>
> Dogs are fairly expensive to keep, **whereas** cats usually cost very little. **Moreover**, dogs need training, exercise, play and even baths, **while** cats, **on the other hand**, can look after themselves.
>
> **However**, the pleasure that a dog can give a lonely person is probably greater, since cats, **although** nice to hold and stroke, can be a little too independent. They are certainly not as 'loving' as dogs, and they have some rather unpleasant habits, such as bringing small dead birds and animals (or parts of them) into the house. Dogs, **in contrast**, provide real companionship. They may help their owner to become friendly with other dog-owners, and they can also guard a home against burglars.
>
> **On balance**, I would say that for an old lady an appropriate breed of dog is a more suitable companion than a cat.

 Exercise 38

Write out two tables for the following: A car or a bike? Which is more suitable for travelling in cities?

Cars	
Good points (+)	**Bad points (−)**

Bikes	
Good points (+)	**Bad points (−)**

Exercise 39

Below are some composition titles. They ask for

a) advantages and disadvantages (like 'Air Travel') or
b) your opinion (like 'Old People') or
c) a general discussion (like 'Cat or Dog') or
d) suggestions for solving a problem.

Following the patterns given before each of the three sample answers, write down your *notes* (not complete sentences) and *ideas* for each title. The letter (a), (b), (c) or (d) after each title shows which of the above-mentioned types of composition is required:

1 Do you think marriage is a good idea? If so, say why; if not, say why not. (b)
2 Discuss the advantages and disadvantages of living in a town. (a)
3 Books or the radio. If you had to live without one of these which one would it be? Say why. (c)
4 Our seas, rivers and lakes are becoming dirtier. What do you think can be done about this? (d)
5 Boys should receive a different type of education from that received by girls. What is your opinion on this? Give your reasons. (b)
6 What are the advantages and disadvantages of having some form of censorship for television? (a)

How to make a point or express an opinion or reason

The following list of phrases includes those printed in bold in the sample answers on pages 66–7.

- First of all...
- One advantage / One disadvantage } of (air travel) is...
- Another point in favour of (air travel) is...
  Another point against (air travel) is...
- A further argument { in favour of / against } ...
- One other advantage / One other disadvantage } is...
- The biggest advantage / The biggest disadvantage } is...
- One objection to this argument is...
- This is not always the case (means 'not always true')
- Take for instance... (means 'here is an example')
- In my opinion, (dogs are more suitable)...
- I think (the state) should (be responsible for...)
- If (an old person is)..., then...
- It's important/true/necessary to remember/point out that...
- Bearing this in mind, I think... (means 'remembering what I've just said')
- It is worth remembering that...
- To sum up / On balance } I would say that...

How to link the points or opinions or reasons together

The following phrases include those printed in bold in the sample answers on pages 66–7.

△ *Note:* After some phrases you will see (+) or (−) symbols. These are to show you whether the points being expressed should be 'positive' or 'negative' ones.

On the one hand..., on the other hand...

- *On the one hand* travelling by air is very fast; *on the other hand* it has several disadvantages.

This is the full expression but the second part is more easily used alone. It is used to introduce an opposite point.

But

- There are many advantages in owning a dog, *but* there are one or two disadvantages too.

In contrast

- Cats are rather independent. Dogs, *in contrast*, provide real companionship.
  This is a less common alternative to 'on the other hand'.

Besides (+ +) or (− −)

- *Besides* this problem, there is the question of exercise for dogs. (− −)
- *Besides* providing financial help for old people, the government should build more special homes (+ +)

This is used to add one point, advantage, problem, question to another.

Moreover (+ +) or (− −)

- Air travel is easy, comfortable and quick. *Moreover*, it is relatively cheap. (+ +)

This is used to add one point to another.

Whereas; while (+ −) or (− +)

- Dogs are fairly expensive to keep, *whereas* cats cost very little. (− +)
- Dogs must be taken for walks, *while* cats can look after themselves. (− +)

This is used to link two opposing ideas on the same subject.

However; although; in spite of

See 1 Telling a Story, page 39.

Exercise 40

Look at the ideas you wrote down for the subjects in Exercises 36, page 66, and 37, page 67. Using the ways of making a point and expressing an opinion write the ideas in complete sentences.

Example:
One advantage of television is that it helps to keep people well-informed.

Exercise 41

Using the ways of linking points or opinions or reasons (page 68) complete the following:

1. Football is an exciting game.
   Cricket, in contrast, _____.
2. People say that living in a foreign country is difficult.
   On the other hand it _____.
3. People from northern countries tend to be rather reserved.
   Those from Mediterranean countries, on the other hand _____.
4. England has a monarchy, whereas _____
5. In England we drive on the left, while _____.
6. Our currency is pounds sterling, whereas _____.
7. England has no compulsory military service, but _____.
8. There are no really high mountains in England, whereas _____.
9. Besides killing conversation, television _____.
10. Gardens provide a place for children to play. Moreover, they _____.

Exercise 42

Look at the notes you wrote down for the subjects in Exercise 39, page 68. Choose one title and expand these notes into a complete composition of between 120 and 180 words.

10 A talk or speech

A question requiring you to write a speech or talk will give a certain amount of information to help you with your ideas.

Example:
You have been asked to talk to a group of young people about a leisure-time activity that interests you. Write what you would say to them.

You therefore know about your subject (leisure-time activity) and your audience (a group of young people). However, at this stage it is useful to consider adding a little more detail:

- what *is* your leisure-time activity?
  – is it skiing, playing the violin, or making model cars, for example?
- who *are* the young people you are talking to?
  – are they members of a club? do they know something about your activity or
- will it be completely new to them?

So, before you start writing the composition, you should have worked out that, for example, you are going to talk about skiing to a group of young people who have never experienced it, but who are interested in finding out about the sport because they may want to take it up as a hobby.

 Exercise 43

Look at the following two questions, in which you are asked to write speeches. In each case, write down as many extra details as you can (e.g. who you are speaking to, what the presents/prizes concerned are, exactly what the competition was, what the colleague was well known or popular for, and where he is going to live and why).

1 You have won a prize in a competition (for sport, music, etc.). Write the speech you make when you accept the prize.

2 You have been asked to present a leaving present to a colleague who is going abroad to live. Write the speech you make at the farewell party.

Below are some phrases which can be used in different kinds of talks and speeches. You will find some of the phrases being used in the sample answer on page 71 where they have been printed in bold type.

Useful phrases

Beginning

- Good evening, ladies and gentlemen...
- I'm sure you all know why we are here.
- It's very nice to see you all here today.
- The purpose of this meeting is to...
- I am here today to...
- First of all,...
- I'd like to tell you something about...

Introducing someone

- It gives me great pleasure to introduce Mr Sladeworthy, who...
- May I introduce our guest tonight, Mr Sladeworthy.

Welcoming

- I'd like to welcome you all to...
- Welcome, everyone, to...

General remarks

- Speaking personally, I...
- I shall always remember/be grateful for/think of her as a...

Presenting

- On behalf of everyone here, I have great pleasure in presenting this... to...
- I am very happy to present... with this... as a small token of our respect/thanks/gratitude.

Thanking

- I should like to thank everyone for...
- I should like to take this opportunity to say thank you for...
- I am very touched to receive your best wishes.

Giving information

- Today is a very special/sad/happy occasion.
- Today marks the end/beginning of...
- First of all, I'm going to tell you something about...

Saying goodbye

- I/we would like to say how sorry I am/we are to be leaving.
- I/we would like to say how sorry I am/we are that you are leaving.
- I/we would like to wish you good luck for the future.

Concluding

- If anyone wants to ask any questions, I'll do my best to answer.
- I would like to finish by saying ...
- In conclusion, I ...
- Thank you for being so attentive.
- Well, I think that's all I can tell you.

> **Sample question**
> As a pupil at the Griffon School you have been asked to present a small gift to a teacher who is retiring from the school, and to make a short speech at the farewell party.

> **Sample answer**
> **I am quite sure you all know why** I have asked for your attention for a moment, and what I am going to say. Although we are all enjoying ourselves very much here tonight, it is impossible to forget that **this is really a rather sad occasion**, as **it marks the end** not only **of** the term, but also of Mrs Drake's time at our school.
>
> She came to the Griffon School when it was founded in 1956, and has always been one of its best and most popular teachers. **Speaking personally**, but I am sure also **for** many generations of pupils, I must say that she has been a friend to her students as well as a teacher; **I shall always be grateful for** the help and guidance she has given me.
>
> I feel sure **you would like me, on your behalf, to wish her all the very best for her retirement, and I have great pleasure in presenting this small gift as a token of our thanks for all she has given the school.**

Exercise 44

You, as the new wife/husband, have to make a speech at the party after your wedding to thank everybody.

1. First, add a little more detail – who are you thanking, and what for?
2. Then, by looking at the phrases on pages 70–71, decide
   how to start
   how to welcome everyone
   how to give information about yourself and your new wife/husband
   how to thank people
   how to make any general remarks
   how to conclude
3. Finally, write the speech you make.

Exercise 45

Write the speech of thanks and farewell that Mrs Drake makes after the presentation (see sample answer above).

Exercise 46

You have been asked to tell a local travel club about your last holiday. Write the lecture or talk you would give them.

11 Final notes on composition titles

1 In this part of the book (page 37 onwards) you have practised writing compositions under headings such as *Telling a story*, and *Descriptions*. In an actual examination paper, it may not immediately be clear from the question exactly what 'type' of composition you are being asked to write. Words such as 'report' and 'describe' can mean different things in different contexts.

Examples:
'Write a report of an accident' means 'tell the story'.
'Write a report on a restaurant' means 'describe the restaurant, its food, etc.'.
'Describe what happened . . .' means 'tell the story'.
'Describe the scene . . .' means 'describe the place and the people, and then tell the story'.

2 It is also quite likely that in an examination paper you will be faced with questions which *combine* two or even more of the 'types' of composition you have practised: examples of this are the last example above (which would combine descriptive writing with telling a story) and the sample question and answer on page 54, which combined a description of a watch with the story of how it disappeared.

Here are some more composition titles where, for one or both of the reasons given above, you should think carefully about what kind of composition you are going to write. Write the compositions, referring back where it is helpful to the relevant sections in this part of the book. The first two compositions have been done for you as examples, and the third one has some notes which you can use to help you write the report.

Sample question A
Describe a famous sporting occasion in your country.

Sample answer A
May the Fifth is a day everyone in Puritania looks forward to. It's the day when the final of the national football championship is played in Prutown Stadium. The match itself begins at 4.00 p.m. but people go to the stadium long before that to watch and join in the pre-match entertainment.

There are gymnastics exhibitions, music provided by a live group which usually gets people in a good mood, dancing by young men who then invite female spectators to join in, and lots of other things all building up to the kick-off at 4.00 p.m.

Once the game itself has begun, there are ninety minutes of excitement, with the crowd of about 100,000 cheering or booing every move. The atmosphere in the stadium is fantastic and normally not aggressive – somehow the fact that it is a national holiday keeps everyone in a happy mood. At the end of the match, the supporters of the winning team leave the stadium to celebrate the result while the losing supporters go to celebrate the national holiday! Everyone has something to be happy about on May the Fifth.

△ *Note:* This composition combines setting the scene for the event and describing the action and atmosphere. It is written in the present tense because you are asked to describe the sporting occasion in general terms; you are not describing a specific visit (this, of course would be written in the past tense – 'Last Saturday I went to watch the football championship finals.').

COMPOSITION

Sample question B
Write an entry for a travel brochure describing any town you know. You should include some historical detail, suggestions about places to visit and things to do, etc.

Sample answer B
Bamley is a historic market town set in beautiful countryside. It is ideally situated, being only one hour away from the capital but among the hills of Fenshire.

In the town there is lots to do and see: for a start, what about a visit to the market, held every day in the ancient, narrow streets around the town centre? While you are there, pop in to the town museum – it's full of objects and stories from Bamley's past and is well worth a visit.

During the summer there are open-air concerts in the park. Concerts, films, plays, even discos – whatever you want you will find in Bamley.

Then there are some interesting trips to be taken into the surrounding countryside. Just half an hour's drive will take you to the Brown Hills and the magnificent scenery in the National Park there. If you go west from Bamley you can spend an enjoyable day exploring the many old villages around Hudcaster.

Bamley really *is* a perfect place for those who enjoy the old, country way of life.

△ *Note:* This is clearly a descriptive composition. However, the style that you use is determined by the people you are writing for, in this case, readers of the travel brochure. You have to try and make the readers want to come to your town. You therefore need to use more persuasive language.

Sample question C
Write a report for your college magazine on a new restaurant that has opened in your town.

Notes for sample answer C

Details of the place	What's its name? Where is it situated? How many customers can it hold? Who's the owner/manager? What's the decoration like?
Details of food and cost	Is there much variety? Is it well cooked? Are some things better than others? Is it good value? Is there enough food?
Details of service	Are the waiters helpful, courteous? Is the food hot and well-presented? Are the tables and cutlery clean?
Conclusion	What's your final opinion of it?

 Exercise 47

Now write some of the following compositions yourself. Remember to refer back (where it is helpful) to the sections between pages 37 and 71 on the different kinds of composition.

1. Describe the preparations for a public festival in your country, or a country you know well.
2. Give a talk to your local travel society on a journey that you made recently.
3. Write a letter to a friend describing the town you are living in and the work you are now doing.
4. Write a description of a concert you attended, for a music society magazine.
5. Describe the scene when a famous politician visited your college.
6. Write a report for a student magazine about a new nightclub in your town.
7. Describe how the present-day system of government or law works in your country (or a country of your choice).
8. Write a report for an insurance company telling them details of how some property was stolen from your room, and describe the missing articles.
9. Give a brief account of the life of a famous person (real or imaginary).
10. Write a short history of your home town or area, up to about the time you were born.
11. Describe the preparations for a wedding in your country.

PAPER 3
Use of English

INTRODUCTION

This paper comprises 'open completion or transformation items' (see 1–7), which are 'designed to test active control of the language at an appropriate communicative level'. There is normally also a 'directed writing' exercise (see 8 and 9), whose aim is 'to test ability to interpret and present information'.

Some types of question (particularly 1 and 2) appear regularly from year to year; other types may be set in alternative examinations or less frequently. There are usually five or six questions in the paper, ending with one of the types of 'directed writing' tests shown in 8 and 9. The sections which follow give practice in all the kinds of question which have been set since 1975.

		page
1	Filling in the blanks in a passage	77
2	Sentence transformation	81
3	Changing the form of words in context	108
4	Guided sentence writing	110
5	Incomplete dialogues	111
6	Indirect and direct speech	112
7	Vocabulary and phrasal verb questions	114
8	Questions based on dialogue or texts	116
9	Questions based on other source material	120

USE OF ENGLISH

1 Filling in the blanks in a passage

Points to remember

1 Read the whole passage at least once to get the general meaning.

2 Look at the words surrounding each blank, especially (but not only) those in the same sentence, to find anything which can help you decide the *meaning* and *grammatical form* of the missing word.

Example 1:
He woke up even _____ tired than the previous day.
('than' indicates a comparative).
Answer: more

Example 2:
Although I have _____ actually seen him, I have watched him on TV.
('although' indicates that there is opposition between the two halves of the sentence.)
Answer: never

Example 3:
He was _____ fed up with working in the same old boring job.
(the sentence is complete in meaning so the word for the blank must be a way of describing 'fed up'.)
Answer: totally/completely

3 When you have completed the text, look very carefully at each word that you have written and ask yourself:
 • Does it have a logical meaning in its sentence and in the passage as a whole? (see Exercise 1)
 • Is it grammatically correct? (see Exercise 2)

Exercise 1

In each of the following sentences the word in italics is wrong: it is grammatically correct but its meaning does not take account of its surroundings. Say what the correct word should be in each case.

Example:
The grass is very rich, *but* the cows quickly become fat.
Answer: and ('but' introduces something which is in opposition to what has gone before)

1 This might have sounded comparatively easy. In fact, it was quite the *same*.

2 Mary lived in Belford and James lived and worked in the surrounding countryside. So, every evening at six o'clock, he walked *from* the town to meet her.

3 We're definitely going for a picnic *if*, of course, it rains. I'm looking forward to a nice relaxing day in the sun.

4 The man who opened the door said *hello* at first, but just stood and stared at us.

5 I told him that when he was driving my car he must *never* wear his seat belt, to protect him from possible injury.

6 'Oh no!' she exclaimed. 'Can't you stay *here*! I'm tired of seeing you here every day.'

7 I'd *love* to go on holiday with her; she's so bad-tempered I'm sure we should argue all the time.

8 When we reached the forest we walked *through* it to avoid the wild animals and other dangers that we knew it contained.

9 The wood was full of *trees*, which ran away as we approached.

10 He was an excellent swimmer and tennis player, and was *not* very good at golf.

11 I went for a walk in the country which surrounds *a* town where I live.

12 He was kneeling down in front of the fireplace, *reading* a newspaper to light the fire with.

Exercise 2

In each of the following sentences the word in italics is wrong: it is 'correct' in meaning, but grammatically impossible in its context. Say what the correct word should be in each case.

Example:
I have many *friend* in Oxford.
Answer: friends ('friend' should be plural, following 'many')

1 I am very fond of *listen* to music.

2 When I got home everybody *is* watching TV.

3 I was so tired I went home and *laid* on the bed for half an hour.

4 We have *any* bread in the house.

5 He looked *as* a ghost.

6 There was hardly *no* work to do in the factory.

7 It was *so* nice weather we went for a walk.
8 She did the new exercise even more *careful* than the last one.
9 '*Who's* is this?' he asked.
10 He is always tired because he works *hardly*.

△ *Note:* There are two areas of language to which you should pay particular attention at this point, since they are regularly tested in blank-filling exercises of this kind. The first involves constructions with auxiliary verbs (must, should, ought, have, can, could, may, might, etc.)

Examples:
John felt very guilty when he remembered that he should _____ been at home instead of at the cinema. (have)
There was nobody in the house, but the fire was still burning. The detective realised that the occupants _____ have left in a hurry. (must)

The second area of language involves relative pronouns, or the lack of them! (which, who, whose, etc.)

Examples:
Suzanne, _____ was born in the USA, has been working here since July. (who)
_____ we saw really made us angry. (What)
She said she was busy, _____ was a lie. (which)
A car _____ brakes are faulty is a dangerous vehicle. (whose)
The chair I was sitting _____ began to move. (on)
The man _____ car belonged to was away on holiday. (the)
The town _____ I was born has the largest fish and chip shop in the world. (where)

Exercise 3

In this exercise, decide which word fits best into the blank.
Remember to check for: correct meaning
                       correct grammar

1 I walked out of _____ front door and closed it behind me.
  A a B the
2 Don't forget to put _____ books away.
  A this B these C that
3 There was _____ left in the cupboard.
  A anything B nothing
4 I never seem to have _____ time to play tennis.
  A much B many C few

5 Homework is optional – you _____ not do it.
  A need B must
6 He took them away although I insisted they were _____.
  A our B ours C his
7 When I told _____ the results, she cried.
  A she B he C her
8 Look! There are his footprints. He _____ have gone this way.
  A can B must C ought
9 The boy played with the scissors and cut _____ so badly that he was taken to hospital.
  A himself B him
10 Francis: The weather's going to be warm tomorrow.
   Jenny: I certainly hope _____ I want to go swimming
   A not B so
11 I stayed at the Dorchester Hotel, _____ is the most expensive hotel in London.
   A that B which
12 There are a lot of things to do in London, _____ going to museums.
   A like B as C by
13 Mike Cobb, _____ home was in Chilton, left the carriage at Didcot.
   A who B that C whose
14 She looked in the cupboard, but couldn't see anything _____.
   A here B in C there
15 Although it was _____ cold, she decided to go for a swim.
   A rather B not
16 Don't worry. Your mother will be here _____.
   A soon B now
17 _____ I really can't understand is the ending of the film.
   A That B What
18 I really don't like the theatre so I _____ go.
   A always B never
19 James looked _____ the window and saw a man at his gate.
   A through B up C out
20 _____ he was angry, he listened to me patiently.
   A However B In spite of C Although
21 'Romeo and Juliet', _____ you are going to see tomorrow, was written by Shakespeare.
   A that B which C what

22 _____ he opened the door, a big hairy dog jumped out.
A As B While

23 I can't stand either Bach _____ Beethoven.
A nor B or C either

24 I came to the conclusion that _____ would persuade me to work in that place again. I had finished there for ever.
A nothing B anything C something

25 We won't be able to go _____ we can find some money.
A if B unless

26 It was _____ good to be working again that he willingly stayed to do overtime.
A too B so

 Exercise 4

Put *one* suitable word in each of the following blanks. Read through the story carefully before beginning to answer.

Albert Schweitzer went to Gabon in 1913 (1) _____ a doctor, together with his wife. He wanted to help, in a practical (2) _____, people who were not (3) _____ fortunate as himself. He was (4) _____ man with many talents and qualifications. When he began his medical studies (5) _____ the age of 30 he already (6) _____ three doctorates – in philosophy, theology and music. Music was a passion throughout (7) _____ life and his talent for playing the piano and organ (8) _____ him to raise money for the Schweitzer hospital in Gabon. His first hospital, (9) _____ he helped to build, attracted patients with a variety of diseases. Today's modern hospital, built (10) _____ to the original one, looks (11) _____ the same sort of patients. (12) _____ Albert Schweitzer died in 1965, his work goes (13) _____, as does his belief (14) _____ 'reverence for life', which is still the guiding principle at the hospital in Gabon.

 Exercise 5

Put *one* suitable word in each of the following blanks. Read through the story carefully before beginning to answer.

The morning train seemed more crowded (1) _____ passengers than usual. As I pushed through them I resigned (2) _____ to standing for most of the tedious journey to the town, but as the train drew (3) _____ of the station, I noticed (4) _____ empty seat (5) _____ distance away, by a window. I glanced cautiously around, but (6) _____ of the other passengers seemed to (7) _____ observed it; so with a show of indifference I (8) _____ for the seat and sat down. Opposite me (9) _____ a boy of about eleven years of age. He was playing with a small object, (10) _____ he was allowing to run over his hands and arms. A small toy, no doubt; but I looked again and it was (11) _____ that I realised why I had gained the seat so easily – (12) _____ small object was a large spider.

 Exercise 6

Write five simple sentences (check with your teacher that they are correct!) and then take out one word from each. In class give one sentence to another student and ask him to supply the missing word. Afterwards, discuss any problems that arose.

Exercise 7

Find a piece of written English which is not too difficult and take out every fifth word. Bring it to class and exchange passages with your neighbour, and fill in the gaps in each other's texts.

△ *Note:* The way in which you need to think when trying to find a suitable word with which to fill a blank is very similar to the way you practised on pages 12–19 (*Finding the meaning of unknown words*). If a word is unknown to you, or if there is a blank instead of a word, you have to use the context around the word/blank to help you make an intelligent guess.

 Exercise 8

Put *one* suitable word in each of the following blanks. There will be some words in the text that you won't understand but this should not affect your understanding of the general meaning of the passage.

Keith (1) _____ downstairs and started looking (2) _____ the analyn. He knew he (3) _____ left it (4) _____, but where? There were only a few possible places; the thing was (5) _____ big that it wouldn't fit just (6) _____. He was worried if it (7) _____ be all right because analyns (8) _____ famous for zetching after a while. He knew that (9) _____ he found it soon it would have zetched, and Rosie would have to spend (10) _____ cleaning the mess (11) _____. He had had this (12) _____ analyn for (13) _____ time and he was really rather fond (14) _____ it. (15) _____ he remembered the (16) _____ the analyn salesman had given him. If you lose (17) _____ analyn you must report it to the authorities. They would then send a trander-man to you, (18) _____ would help you to locate it. (19) _____ he contacted the authorities and they promised to see (20) _____ it immediately.

Like *sprill* and *wungle* on pages 12–13, *analyn*, *zetching* and *trander-man* are nonsense words which do not exist in English. They are included to remind you:

- that you can understand the general sense of a passage even without knowing all the words.
- that even though the three words above cannot be found in any dictionary, their function is clear in their context; and when reading the text you probably gave them 'meanings' in your own mind.

2 Sentence transformation

The *Use of English* paper usually contains an exercise which involves the 'transformation' or 'conversion' of one sentence into a differently worded sentence, with as nearly as possible the same meaning. In this type of question the instructions to the student are usually 'Finish each of the following sentences in such a way that it means exactly the same as the sentence printed before it'.

Example:
I haven't enjoyed myself so much for years.
It's years _____.

Answer: It's years since I enjoyed myself so much.

An exercise of this type tests your ability to use the structures of English, and a good knowledge of English grammar is essential: you should refer to your English Grammar when a point arises about which you are not clear.

In the following pages you will find notes and practice exercises on many structural points which can be tested by means of 'conversion exercises'. In most cases each 'half' of the conversion is practised in turn before the two parts are put together into a conversion exercise. For example, the section on passive-active forms begins with examples of passive forms and exercises in forming the passive, continues with examples of active forms, and ends with work practising conversions from one to the other.

This section does not aim to provide a comprehensive survey of English grammar, but is intended to focus your attention on problem areas and on the kinds of structure that you need to master in order to pass the First Certificate Examination. The constructions dealt with are the following:

	page
Passive-active forms	81
Causative 'have'	87
Make/let/allow	88
-ing/-ed	89
Transitive/intransitive uses of verbs	89
If/unless	89
If only/I wish	91
In case	92
Direct/indirect speech	92
It's time	95
Concealed relatives	96
Must not/needn't/Don't have to	96
For/since/ago	97
Still/yet	98
Noun or verb	98
So do I/I do too/nor can I neither can I/I can't either	99
Comparison	99
Comparative/superlative	100
So/such, etc.	100
'Uncountables'	102
Adverbs/adjectives	102
Prefer/would rather/would prefer	103
Miscellaneous	103

Passive-active forms

For testing purposes, you are often asked to transfer sentences from the active to the passive, or the other way round. Sometimes this kind of transfer produces artificial sentences, but it is a good way of testing your ability to manage the construction.

Examples:
Oil has been found in Scotland. (passive)
People have found oil in Scotland. (active)

The first sentence is more natural because it gives the information that is necessary – oil/found/Scotland. The second sentence sounds rather artificial ('people' adds nothing to the meaning).

This section has been divided into:

- Passive forms
- Active forms
- How to make the conversion
- Practice in conversion
- Special cases (impersonal 'it')
- 'Needs' with the gerund

Passive forms

After each of the following examples of the various forms of the passive in English there is a sentence (marked *) for you to complete using the same tense as the example. From the information given on the left, note carefully how each sentence is formed.

Present simple
(am/is/are
+ past participle)

Rover cars *are made* in Oxford.
*Although the British car industry has had its problems, large numbers of vehicles _____. (still sell/every year)

Present perfect
(has/have
+ been + past participle)

Gold *has been discovered* in a garden in East Oxford.
*The police _____. (not yet/inform)

Past simple
(was/were
+ past participle)

The runaway girl *was found* living in a commune in Liverpool.
*Unwillingly, she _____. (take back/to her home in Glasgow)

Future
(will be + past participle)

You*'ll be told* what to do when you arrive.
*On Monday, if you are still here, you _____. (give/uniform)

Past Perfect
(had been + past participle)

When I arrived at the scene of the accident, the cars *had* already *been removed*.
*Luckily, two eye-witnesses _____. (find)

'Going to' future
(am/is/are
+ going to be
+ past participle)

I'm afraid you*'re going to be disappointed* by the examination results.
*The headmaster says that you _____. (remove/from the school)

Past continuous
(was/were being
+ past participle)

We don't know the result of the election yet. The votes *were* still *being counted* when I last telephoned.
*When I rang again later they had finished counting, but the final result _____. (still/check)

Present continuous
(am/is/are
being + past participle)

We can't use this room, I'm afraid – it*'s being redecorated* at the moment.
*In fact, the whole design of the room _____. (change)

Present continuous with future meaning
(am/is/are
being + past participle)

The race meeting next Saturday *is being sponsored by* a firm of rubber manufacturers.
*This means that because of objections by the BBC, no races _____. (televise)

Present infinitive
((to) be + past participle)

Is found after auxiliary verbs (*can, could, may, might, must, would, ought to, should, used to*), and after verbs which are always or sometimes followed by the infinitive (*expect to, want to, have (got) to, would like to, would prefer to, intend to, agree to, refuse to, arrange to, manage to, decide to*, etc.).

Examples:
Something's *got to be done*.
Nothing *can be done*.
He knew that if he stayed there he *would be eaten*.
He *ought to be told* about it.
You *may be stopped* by the police if you go out wearing that!
I *want* you *to be known* all over the world.
I *would prefer to be examined* by a lady doctor, please.
They *arranged to be picked* up from the airport at six o'clock.
*Perhaps for a change the students should _____ (ask) to give their own opinions.
*That animal must, at all costs, _____. (recapture)
*Room service? I'd like _____. (wake up/at eight o'clock)
*I certainly don't intend _____. (frighten/by him)

Past infinitive
((to) have been
+ past participle)

Is found after auxiliary verbs (see list above), and after a few verbs which are followed by the infinitive.

USE OF ENGLISH

Examples:
I suppose the missing money *might have been taken* from my pocket.
This book *must have been written* ages ago – it's terribly out of date.
Jim probably won't be here at Christmas – he *hopes to have been transferred* to London by then.
*He spent the evening with me, so he can't _____.
(see/near the bank/by the police/at nine o'clock)
*That job ought _____.
(finish/hours ago)

Participle
(being + past participle)

Occurs after verbs of sensation like *see, hear, feel*.

Example:
I saw my car *being towed* away from the parking meter.
*I heard the door _____.
(push) open.

Gerund
(being + past participle)

Occurs after verbs which are always or sometimes followed by the gerund, such as *remember, avoid, enjoy, prefer, dread, stop, admit, mind,* etc. and after *prepositions*.

Examples:
I remember *being told* never to use the word 'nice'.
Do you mind *being left* out of the team on Saturday?
After *being dismissed* by his firm, he went steadily downhill.
*She enjoys _____.
(take out/to dinner)

Exercise 9

Complete the following sentences by filling in the correct form of the passive with the verbs shown.

Read the sentence carefully to find out the required tense of the verb. If you are not sure of the form, refer to pages 82–3.

Example:
The train _____ (delay) by fog last night.
Answer: The train was delayed by fog last night.

1 He _____ already _____ (knock off) his bike several times before last week's accident.
2 I _____ just _____ (tell) that I've passed my examination!
3 Library fines must _____ (pay) to the lady by the door.
4 The boy _____ (send) to school in America next year.
5 The window _____ (repair) at the moment.
6 A message _____ just _____ (receive) from headquarters.
7 The problem can _____ (solve) by a computer.
8 When Mrs Penn went back to her hotel room after breakfast, it still _____ (clean).
9 What happened to President Lincoln? He _____ (shoot).
10 I remember _____ (take) to the zoo by my father when I was little.

Active forms

Look back to the examples on pages 82–3 and compare the passive verb forms with the active forms in italics below.

Present simple	The workers who are on strike in Oxford *make* Rover cars.
Present perfect	A ninety-year-old grandmother *has discovered* gold in her garden in East Oxford.
Past simple	The parents of sixteen-year-old Valerie Carpenter, who ran away from her home last month, *found* her living in a commune in Liverpool yesterday.
Future	The guide will meet you at the airport and she *will tell* you what to do.
Past perfect	The policeman told me that the Swan Garage *had removed* the cars from the scene of the accident.
'Going to' future	The results of your exam have just come in and I'm afraid they're *going to disappoint* you.

Past continuous	Poor old Terry had no sleep last night. He *was* still *counting* the votes at three o'clock in the morning.
Present continuous	My wife is a do-it-yourself enthusiast. Last week she did the kitchen and this week she's *redecorating* the bedroom.
Present continuous with future meaning	The rubber company who *are sponsoring* next Saturday's race meeting at Brand's Hatch have made a huge profit this year.
Present infinitive	Our rubbish hasn't been collected for weeks. The local authority *has got to do* something about it.
Past infinitive	I've just thought! That man who bumped into me in the street *might have taken* the money from my pocket.
Participle	I arrived just in time to see the police *towing* my car away.
Gerund	I remember my teacher *telling* me never to use the word 'nice'.

In the following two newspaper reports, put the verbs in brackets into the correct form (passive or active) and correct tense.

Exercise 10

Bradchester Football Club's dynamic young manager, Emlyn Jones, **(1)** _____ (sack). The news **(2)** _____ (come) last night in an interview with our reporter. Mr Jones **(3)** _____ (say) that he and the directors of the club **(4)** _____ (disagree) about how things should be done. He **(5)** _____ (ask) by the directors to sell three players, and although he **(6)** _____ (not like) doing this, he agreed. In fact, one of the players, Tom Keegan, **(7)** _____ (buy) by a German club only yesterday.

At yesterday's game Emlyn Jones's team **(8)** _____ (beat) at home by Brownpool and after the match the directors **(9)** _____ (tell) by Mr Jones that the defeat **(10)** _____ (be) a direct result of selling the three players. It **(11)** _____ (be) at this point that Mr Jones **(12)** _____ (tell) to leave the club.

Today **(13)** _____ (be) a sad day for Bradchester and a happy day for some other club. There is no doubt that Emlyn Jones **(14)** _____ (offer) another job very soon, and we **(15)** _____ (wish) him luck.

Exercise 11

Last night strong winds and heavy rain **(1)** _____ (bring) chaos to the area. Trees **(2)** _____ (blow down), rivers **(3)** _____ (burst) their banks and large areas of the countryside around Milton **(4)** _____ (flood). This is the second time this month that Milton **(5)** _____ (flood). Our reporter **(6)** _____ (fly) over the area early this morning and **(7)** _____ (see) at least thirty cars which **(8)** _____ (abandon). Farmers in the affected area reported that many cattle and sheep **(9)** _____ (drown), and for those that **(10)** _____ (survived), the problem is now food. One motorist **(11)** _____ (have) a lucky escape last night when a tree **(12)** _____ (fall) across the road, and **(13)** _____ (land) on the bonnet of his car. Emergency services in the area **(14)** _____ (work) through the night to rescue motorists, and many abandoned cars **(15)** _____ (tow away). Motorists **(16)** _____ (ask) by the police to check with local garages if their cars **(17)** _____ (disappear)!

How to make the conversion

Active to passive

Example:
They produce excellent wine in Italy.

1 Find the *object* of the sentence and make it the new *subject*:
   'Excellent wine...'
2 Decide the tense of the original verb: present simple.
3 Write the same tense of the verb 'to be': 'is'.
4 Add the past participle of the main verb: 'produced'.
5 Decide if the original subject or agent is necessary. If it is, put 'by...'; if not, forget it.
6 Any other information? – 'in Italy'.
7 Sentence: 'Excellent wine is produced in Italy.'

USE OF ENGLISH

Passive to active

Example:
All the TV aerials had been blown down by the wind.

1 Find the agent and make it the new subject: 'The wind'. (If there is no agent, you will have to create one, e.g. 'they', 'someone', 'people'.)
2 Decide what tense of the verb 'to be' has been used: past perfect.
3 Write the same tense of the verb 'to blow': 'had blown'.
4 Make passive subject into active object: 'all the TV aerials'.
5 Sentence: 'The wind had blown down all the TV aerials.'

Practice in conversion

 Exercise 12

Convert the following active sentences into passive constructions. Only put in the agent when you think it is necessary:

Example:
I've told her many times not to do that.
She _____

Answer: She *has been told* many times not to do that.

1 The guide took us round the palace.
   We _____.
2 When I passed this morning, some workmen were repairing the road.
   When I passed this morning, the road _____.
3 Since my last visit, they have redecorated the house.
   Since my last visit, the house _____.
4 The Japanese export a wide variety of goods.
   A wide variety of goods _____.
5 The multi-national company should take over the unprofitable one.
   The unprofitable company _____.
6 We used to cover car seats in leather but now we cover them in plastic.
   Car seats used _____.
7 He hates the teacher giving him extra work.
   He hates _____.
8 I am sure someone will discover the murderer one day.
   I am sure the murderer _____.
9 The police will remove your car if you leave it there.
   Your car _____.
10 The distributors are releasing the new film in New York.
    The new film _____.

 Exercise 13

Convert the following passive sentences into active constructions.

Example:
The employees *were told* by the company director that the company had made a profit that year.
The company director _____.

Answer: The company director *told* the employees that the company had made a profit that year.

1 The new school in Blackpool will be opened by a famous local footballer.
   A famous local footballer _____.
2 She hasn't been told what sort of meal to prepare.
   No-one _____.
3 Mr Simpson said the large hole in the road had been caused by a burst water pipe.
   Mr Simpson said a burst water pipe *had caused the large hole in the road*.
4 Every year millions of tons of good food are thrown away.
   Every year people _____.
5 Traffic is being diverted away from the centre of town by the police.
   The police _____.

6 When I arrived at the farm the cows were being milked.
   When I arrived at the farm someone _____.

7 Those houses are going to be demolished next week by a local contractor.
   A local contractor _____.

8 That door must not be opened!
   You _____.

9 I object to being asked questions in the street.
   I object to people _____.

10 I actually saw my bike being stolen.
   I actually saw someone _____.

Special cases (Impersonal 'it')

Constructions with: *believe, say, think, consider, report, claim, suppose, find, know, acknowledge, understand.*

Construction A

- *It is believed* that he is the only survivor of the disaster.
- *It has been said* that a large monster lives in Loch Ness in Scotland.
- *It was thought* by the local people that the church was haunted.

△ Note: A variety of tenses can be used in each 'half' of the sentence, depending on the situation.

 Exercise 14

Make sentences similar to the examples above from the following information.

Example:
People think/John/a good candidate.
It is thought that John is a good candidate.

1 People claim/too much meat/bad for your health.
   It _____.

2 People say/our weather/changing.
   It _____.

3 People consider/Paris/one of the world's most beautiful cities.
   It _____.

Now compare the three sentences above (Construction A) with the three sentences below (Construction B).

Construction B

- *He is believed to be* the only survivor of the disaster.
- *A large monster has been said to live* in Loch Ness in Scotland.
- *The church was thought* by the local people *to be* haunted.

Variations of tense are also possible with this construction, depending on exactly what time is referred to in each part of the sentence.

 Exercise 15

Make sentences similar to the examples above from the information given here.

Example:
Peter/wonderful tennis-player (suppose)
Peter is supposed to be a wonderful tennis-player.

1 Rob Banks/living in South America (know)
   Rob Banks _____.

2 Segovia/world's finest guitar player (say)
   Segovia _____.

3 The President/have/huge private fortune (understand)
   The President _____.

 Exercise 16

Now change sentences from the form used in Construction A to that in Construction B, or vice versa. Remember to look carefully now for tenses other than the present.

Example 1:
Prince James is known to be interested in cookery.
It _____.

Answer: It *is known* that Prince James is interested in cookery.

Example 2:
People say that Atlantis was destroyed by a huge tidal wave.
Atlantis _____.

Answer: Atlantis *is said to have been* destroyed by a huge tidal wave.

Example 3:
The archaeologists found that the ten-million-year-old skeleton was made of plastic.
The ten-million-year-old skeleton _____.

Answer: The ten-million-year-old skeleton *was found to be* made of plastic.

1 People believe that the Pyramids of Egypt were built without machines.
   The Pyramids of Egypt _____.
2 Some people say that apes can understand human speech.
   Apes _are said to be understood human_ (What is the infinitive of 'can'?) _speech_.
3 Columbus is thought to have discovered America.
   It _is thought C discovered A_
4 The police reported that the car had been found in Bournemouth.
   The car _was reported to have been found in B._
5 Scientists know that man is less hairy than he was centuries ago.
   Man _is known to be less hairy than he was centuries ago._

'Needs' with the gerund

'Needs', when followed by the gerund (-ing), produces a passive meaning.

Examples:
Your hair *needs* cutting. (= it needs to be cut)
What *needs* doing? (= what needs to be done?)

△ Note: 'Wants' is sometimes used in the same way and then has the same meaning as 'needs'.
Her car *wants* washing. (= it needs to be washed)

Exercise 17

Write sentences similar to the examples above from the information given:

1 It's time my house was painted.
   My house needs _____.
2 Someone ought to explain it.
   It needs _____.
3 I wish someone would clean my suit!
   My suit needs _____.

Causative 'have'

Used when we want to say 'I didn't do it; someone else did it for me.'

Example:
Francis: Your hair looks nice.
Jenny: Thanks, *I've just had it cut* (by my hairdresser).

This construction is formed by 'have' (in a variety of tenses):
plus the object (e.g. my hair)
plus past participle (e.g. cut)
plus (if necessary) the agent (e.g. my hairdresser)

Exercise 18

Use the above construction in the correct tenses in the following sentences.

Example:
Jane: Did you make that dress yourself?
Sue: No, I _____ by the dressmaker round the corner.
Answer: had it made.

1 The car is running much better now because I _____ (service) last week.
2 Your hair looks different. _____ (cut)?
3 Her sitting room looks rather a mess so she _____ (redecorate) next week by Mr Brick.
4 My house is so much warmer now, because I _____ central heating (instal).
5 Rob: I feel lost without a watch.
   Ann: Where is it?
   Rob: I _____ (repair) at the moment.
6 We have coal fires in our house, and the chimneys very soon get dirty.
   We have to _____ (sweep) regularly.
7 Your suit looks a mess. Why don't you _____ (clean)?
8 Your car engine sounds terribly rough to me. You really must _____ (check) soon.

9 The tree in my garden is so old it's getting dangerous, so I'm afraid I'll just have to _____ (cut down).

10 That's the second time the heel of my shoe has come off, and I _____ (mend) only last week!

 Exercise 19

Complete the second sentence in each of the following pairs of sentences so that it means the same as the first sentence.

Example:
A man came and serviced my washing machine for me yesterday.
I _____.

Answer: I *had* my washing machine *serviced* yesterday.

1 Mr Clamp repaired my car for me last week.
I _____.

2 They are going to X-ray my knee on Friday.
I'm going to _____.

3 A girl manicures my boss's nails twice a week.
My boss _____.

4 Has anybody ever told your fortune?
Have you *ever had your fortune told*?

5 Lord Snowshill is taking my photograph on Friday.
I*'m having my photograph taken on*

Make/let/allow

Examples:
His mother *made him put* a vest on before he went out. (active)
He *was made to put* a vest on before he went out. (passive)
His mother { didn't / wouldn't } *let him* go out without a vest on. (active)
His mother { didn't / wouldn't } *allow him to* go out without a vest on (active)
He *was not allowed to* got out without a vest on. (passive)

 Exercise 20

Write down three things your mother *made you do* when you were a child. Use the active and then the passive constructions.

Example:
My mother made me go to bed early.
I *was made to* go to bed early.

 Exercise 21

Write down three things your teacher *wouldn't let you do* when you were at school. Use the active and then the passive constructions.

Example:
My teacher wouldn't let me talk in the lesson.
I *was not allowed to* talk in the lesson.

 Exercise 22

Complete the second sentence in each of the following pairs of sentences so that it means the same as the first sentence.

Example 1:
I was not allowed by my parents to eat sweet things.
My parents _____.
Answer: My parents *wouldn't let me* eat sweet things.
or My parents *wouldn't allow me to* eat sweet things.

Notice that in order to keep the meaning of your new sentence as close as possible to the original, you may have to make some additional changes.

Example 2:
The soldiers would not let him go outside the room.
The soldiers made _____.
Answer: The soldiers *made him stay inside* the room.

Example 3:
We are not allowed to attend the lesson if we arrive late.
We are made _____.
Answer: We *are made to miss the lesson* if we arrive late.

1 Our parents made us go to church when we were younger.
We *were made to go to church*.

2 I sent him home.
I made *him go home*.

3 His mother made him go to bed early.
He was not _____.

4 In the last century people were made by the government to join the Navy.
The government _____.

5 The postman wasn't allowed by the dog to go through the gate.
The dog _____.

USE OF ENGLISH

-ing/-ed

Example 1:
The film was very boring for us.
We were _____.
Answer: We *were bored by* the film.

Example 2:
She was depressed by the book.
She found _____.
Answer: She found the book *depressing*.

 Exercise 23

Make similar changes for the following sentences:

1 The news was very exciting for everybody.
  Everybody was very _____.
2 His behaviour was very embarrassing to us.
  We were _____.
3 The students were bored by the lesson.
  The lesson was _____.
4 The results of the examination were disappointing for him.
  He was *disappoint in*
5 We are always interested in Dr Knuckle's lectures.
  We always find _____.

Transitive/intransitive uses of verbs

Verbs used 'transitively' take an object. (The dog bit the man.) Verbs used 'intransitively' have no object. (She was lying on her bed.)
Most common English verbs can be used either transitively or intransitively, sometimes giving different meanings.

Examples:
I *stopped the car.* (transitive)
The car *stopped.* (intransitive)
He *ran his fingers* through my hair. (transitive)
He *ran away* when the police came. (intransitive)
I *rested my elbows* on the table. (transitive)
He *rests* every afternoon after lunch. (intransitive)

Sometimes a transfer can be made directly from an intransitive to a transitive use of a verb, or vice versa, with no significant change of meaning.

 Exercise 24

Look at the examples below and then complete the following five sentences in a similar way.

Example 1:
I run my car on two-star petrol.
My car _____.
Answer: My car *runs* on two-star petrol.

Example 2:
He burnt his hands in the flames.
The flames _____.
Answer: The flames *burnt* his hands.

1 The balloon burst under his weight.
  His weight *burst the balloon.*
2 The shark closed its jaws on the edge of the boat.
  The shark's *jaws closed on the edge of*
3 The door opened silently.
  Someone *opened the door silently*
4 The metal split in the extreme heat.
  The extreme heat *split the metal*
5 My resistance finally broke after hours of questioning.
  The hours of questioning *finally broke my resistance after hours of question*

If/unless

Conditional sentences are difficult and you should refer to your grammar book for detailed explanations of forms, tense changes and meanings.
Study the examples below.

First conditional

Examples:
I'm thinking of going to London at the weekend.
I'll see a show there.
If I go, I'll see a show.

I need to pass this exam. Failure means I won't be able to go to university.

If I don't }
Unless I   } *pass, I won't* be able to go to university.

Exercise 25

Finish the following sentences in your own words:

1 If the weather is good tomorrow, _____.
2 He'll easily get the job if _____.
3 I'm fed up with waiting. I'm leaving if _____ soon.
4 Tom, if you don't listen, you _____.
5 We won't be able to go skiing at the weekend unless _____.

Second conditional

Examples:
I don't know the answer so I can't tell you.
If I knew the answer I *would/could tell* you.

My dream is to sail around the world, but I would need to win a lot of money.
If I won a lot of money I *would sail* round the world.

suppose

 Exercise 26

Answer these questions:

1 What famous person would you like to meet if you had the chance?
 If I _____.
2 What would you do or say if someone stole your purse?
 If someone _____.
3 Where would you live if you could live anywhere in the world?
 If I _____.
4 What three things would you like to do, have or be if you had magic power for a day?
 If I _____.

Third conditional

Look very carefully at the relationship between the negative and positive forms of the verbs in the examples below.

Examples:
He arrived late so he missed the interesting part of the lecture.
If he hadn't arrived late, he *wouldn't have missed* the interesting part of the lecture.
or
If he had arrived early, he *wouldn't have missed* the interesting part of the lecture.

We didn't get lost because we took a map.
We *would have got lost if* we *hadn't taken* a map.

You didn't listen to my suggestion, so now you're in a difficult situation.
If you had listened to my suggestion, you *wouldn't be* in a difficult situation now.

 Exercise 27 ✓

Justin Tyme had an important interview in Liverpool on Tuesday. Unfortunately, he went to bed very late the night before and because he was tired, he forgot to set his alarm clock.

Example:
tired/forgot to set alarm clock.
If he *hadn't been tired*, he *wouldn't have forgotten* to set his alarm clock.

Now, continue the story of Justin's misfortunes in the same way.

1 forget to set clock/wake up early
2 wake up early/catch the 8.00 train
3 catch the 8.00 train/arrive in Liverpool by 10.00
4 arrive in Liverpool by 10.00/get to his interview by 10.30
5 get to interview by 10.30/be offered the job
6 be offered the job/accept it
7 accept the job/earn more money now

USE OF ENGLISH

Exercise 28

This exercise gives you practice in Conditionals 1, 2 and 3. Complete the following sentences in your own words.

1 If you gave me the opportunity, I _____.
2 You'll lose your job if _____.
3 Unless he rings in the next five minutes, I _never_ talk to him
4 She wouldn't have damaged her eyes if _if she had been careful_
5 If we run, we _____.
6 Oh dear, I'm sorry. If I'd known, I _would have_ excited it
7 There's no point in going out tonight unless you _'ve got appointment_
8 If you were famous, _would_ you be happy?
9 If we hadn't missed that train, we _could have arrived by_ now.
10 You would be able to drive a big lorry if you _____.

Exercise 29

This kind of exercise with conditionals will always require some conversion of the verbs from negative to positive or positive to negative to keep the same meaning in your sentence as in the original.

Example 1:
The president made a lot of mistakes, and now he is a private citizen.
If the president _____.
Answer: If the president *hadn't made* a lot of mistakes, he *wouldn't be* a private citizen now.

Example 2:
Say 'please', or I won't give it to you.
If you _____.
Answer: If you *say* 'please', I*'ll give* it to you.
or If you *don't say* 'please', I *won't give* it to you.

1 You can't make an omelette without eggs!
  Unless _____.
2 They didn't understand the film, because they missed the beginning.
  If they _____.
3 We haven't got any matches, so we can't light a fire.
  If we _____.
4 The snack bar round the corner is very cheap, so I eat there for that reason.
  If the snack bar _wasn't so cheap, I wouldn't eat there._

5 I hope it will stop raining, then I can go swimming.
  If it _stops_, I will be able to go swimming
6 I feel terribly sick because I ate so many cream cakes last night.
  If I _hadn't eaten so many cream cakes I wouldn't feel sick._

If only/I wish

Examples:
If only } *I had* some money. (but I haven't)
I wish }

If only } *I could* swim. (but I can't)
I wish }

If only } *I hadn't said* that. (but I did and it's
I wish } too late now)

If only } he *would make* less noise. (but he won't
I wish } and I can't do anything about it)

Exercise 30

Complete the second sentence in each of the following pairs of sentences so that it means the same as the first sentence.

Example:
I should have gone to the party last night. I'm sorry I didn't.
I wish _____.
Answer: I wish I had gone to the party last night.

1 I'd love a car.
  I wish _____.
2 She was really sorry she had married him.
  She wished _____.
3 Rain, rain, rain! Why won't it stop!
  If only it _____!
4 We're lost. Why didn't we bring a map with us?
  I wish we _____.
5 I can't go the party on Saturday, I'm afraid.
  I wish I _____.
6 I would love to live in a hot country where the sun shines every day.
  If only I _____.

In case

'In case' does not mean 'if'. It means 'because there is/was a possibility of something happening'.

Examples:
I'll take an umbrella with me *in case* it rains. (This means I'll take it with me whether it rains or not; 'in case' here explains why I will take it.)

I took some warm clothes *in case* I felt cold.

Look very carefully at the verb tenses in both parts of the sentences.

If the first verb in the sentence is
present
future   } the verb after 'in case' is in the present tense.
present perfect

If the first verb in the sentence is
past   } the verb after 'in case' is usually in
past perfect   the past tense.

Exercise 31

Complete the following sentences in your own words:

1. Put the milk in the fridge in case the cat _____.
2. Motorists carry a spare wheel in case _____.
3. You should never let children play near deep water in case _____
4. When I went sailing I wore a life-jacket in case _____.
5. The climbers took ropes with them in case _____.

Exercise 32

Complete the second sentence in each of the following pairs of sentences so that it means the same as the first sentence.

Example:
I'll take an umbrella with me because *it might rain*.
I'll take an umbrella with me in case _____.

Answer: I'll take an umbrella with me *in case it rains*.

1. Write your address in my book because I might forget it.
   Write your address in my book in case _____.
2. He took a gun with him because he thought he might see some deer.
   He took a gun with him in case _____.
3. He wrote his name and address in the book because he thought someone might take it.
   He wrote his name and address in the book in case _____.
4. Don't forget to take your seasickness pills because you might feel sick crossing the Atlantic.
   Don't forget to take your seasickness pills in case _____.
5. The man opened a Swiss bank account because he thought he might have to leave England quickly!
   The man opened a Swiss bank account in case _____.

Direct/indirect speech

The following are the most important points to remember.

- **Verb tense changes**

  Example:
  'I'*ll see* her later,' he said.
  He said he *would see* her later.

- **Position of verb in question** (see page 93)

  Example:
  'Where'*s* the car?' she asked
  She asked where the car *was*.

- **Use of different introductory verbs,** e.g. warn, suggest, etc. (see page 93)

  Example:
  'Don't go near the fire,' he *said* to her.
  He *warned* her not to go near the fire.

- **Pronoun changes**

  Example:
  'What are *you* doing?' he asked.
  He asked *me/us* what *I/we* were doing.

- **Commands**

  Example:
  'Don't *do* that,' he told me.
  He told me *not to do* that.

- **Temporal changes**

    Example:
    'I'll see you *tomorrow*,' he told me.
    He told me he would see me *the following day*.

Special notes on indirect questions

1 The word order: the main verb is not inverted, as in direct questions.

Example:
'How long *have you* been married?' he asked me.
He asked me how long *I had* been married.

2 The inclusion of 'if' or 'whether' where there is no question word.

Example:
'Do you smoke?' he asked me.
He asked me *if* I smoked.

3 'Hidden' indirect questions introduced by phrases such as 'I wonder' or 'Do you know' or 'I don't know'.

Example:
'When *will they* arrive, I wonder?'
'I wonder when *they will* arrive.'

 Exercise 33

Put the following direct questions into indirect speech.

Example:
'Where's the nearest bus stop?' he asked me.
He asked me _____.

Answer: He asked me where the nearest bus stop was.

1 'What's the time, please?' he asked me.
   He asked me _____.
2 'When did he move here?' the policeman asked her.
   The policeman asked her _____.
3 'Can I see you tomorrow?' she asked him.
   She asked him _____.
4 'How much does it cost to travel to the USA?' she asked the travel agent.
   She asked the travel agent _____.
5 'Was Mr Jones at work today?' the boss asked her secretary.
   The boss asked her secretary _____.

Special note on the use of some introductory verbs

Indirect speech is often known as reported speech and as this name suggests it involves an element of summary.

The verbs below are some of those used as alternatives to 'said' when reporting someone's words. A direct word-for-word conversion from direct to indirect speech is not required, since the introductory verb itself summarises part of what was said.

Warn, recommend, tell, order, advise, invite, encourage, remind, persuade
(+ person + infinitive with 'to')

Examples:
'I think you should stay in the Highland Hotel,' he said.
He *advised* us to stay in the Highland Hotel.

'Don't touch that wire!' he told her.
He *told* her not to touch that wire.

△ *Note:* Some of these verbs can also be followed by other constructions.

Example:
'Don't forget that you haven't paid your bill yet,' he said to us.
He *reminded* us that we had not paid our bill.

Admit . . . ing, deny . . . ing, apologise for . . . ing, accuse him of . . . ing.

Examples:
'I didn't take the money,' he said.
He *denied taking* the money.

'We're sorry we're late,' they said.
They *apologised for* being late.

Suggest

- suggest (+ person + should + infinitive without 'to')

Example:
'I think you'd better stay in bed,' she said.
She *suggested I should stay* in bed.

- suggest + gerund (could include speaker)

Example:
'How about going to the theatre for a change?' she said.
She *suggested going* to the theatre for a change.

Pretend, offer, refuse, promise (+ infinitive)

Examples:
'Don't worry, I'll look after your plants carefully,' she told me.
She *promised to look after* my plants carefully.

'You can't come in, I'm afraid,' the manager said to David.
The manager *refused to let* David in.

Exercise 34

Put the following into indirect speech. Where possible use an introductory verb other than 'said'.

1 'I'm sorry I gave you so much trouble,' she said.
2 'Let's work together and share our ideas,' George said.
3 'I'll carry your case for you,' the young girl said to the man. *offered*
4 'I won't answer your question,' she said to the judge. *refused to answer*
5 'I'll bring the book back tomorrow,' she said. *promised*
6 'I didn't break the plate,' she said. *denied breaking*
7 'You killed her,' the policeman said to Ronald.
8 'Go on, try it,' he said to her. *warn / advised*
9 'I shouldn't do that, if I were you,' her mother said. *advised not to do that*
10 'Would you like to come to the cinema tomorrow?' Ray asked Mildred. *invited to go*
11 'I really think the beef is the best dish on the menu today,' the waiter said to us. *recommended the beef as the best dish / recommended her to buy*
12 'Don't forget to buy Aunt Phyllis a birthday present,' Steve said to Chris.

Exercise 35

Change the following indirect statements into direct speech. Remember that the sentences below are reports of what was said. Try to imagine what words were actually used in these situations.

Example:
He apologised for being late.
'I'm sorry I'm late,' he said.

1 He warned us to leave the snakes alone. *'Leave the snakes alone,' he said*
2 They were told, politely, by the teacher to sit down. *'Would you please sit down,' the teacher said*
3 The manager admitted making a mistake in the accounts. *'Yes, I made a mistake in the accounts,' the manager said*
4 Mrs Honeybone offered Peter a cup of tea. *'Would you like a cup of tea,' Mrs Honeybone said*
5 The hijacker ordered the pilot to return to London Airport. *'Go back to London A'*
6 She refused to leave before the end of the film. *'Won't leave'*
7 She promised to ring me that evening. *'I'll ring you'*
8 The doctor advised him to go to bed. *'You should'*

Exercise 36

Complete each of the following sentences in such a way that it has a similar meaning to that of the sentence printed above it. In each case a transfer from direct to indirect speech, or vice versa, is involved.

Example 1:
'What's the time?' she asked him.
She asked him what _____.

Answer: She asked him what the time was.

Example 2:
He apologised for forgetting her birthday.
'I'm sorry _____.'

Answer: 'I'm sorry I forgot your birthday,' he said.

1 'You have beautiful knees,' he said to her.
He told her that *she had beautiful knees*
2 I asked him to open the door for me.
'Would *you mind opening the door for me*'
3 I told my class that they were lazy and I was not going to teach them any longer.
'You _____.'
4 'You are the man who stole my bicycle!' he said.
He accused me *of stealing his bicycle*
5 'Did you go to the theatre yesterday?' Rosie asked her mother.
Rosie asked her mother *if she had gone to the*
6 'Do you come here often?' she asked him.
She asked him *if he came there often*
7 He reminded her that they hadn't paid the electricity bill.
'Don't forget that *we haven't paid the*' *he said*
8 'Don't play with matches. They're dangerous,' he told her.
He warned her *not to play with matches*
9 'Why don't we stay at home this evening?' Bernard said.
Bernard suggested *that we should stay at home*
10 The travel agent advised him to fly at the weekend.
'I think you _____.'

It's time

Construction A

It's time (+ for + agent) + infinitive with
'to' = the time has come

Examples:
It's time *to go*
It's time *for us to leave*
It's time *for the shop to close/for him to close the shop.*

 Exercise 37

Write sentences using 'It's time (for someone) to _____' from the following:

1 Goodness! Six o'clock already! _____ (shut/shop)
2 Right. Midnight, and that means it's now your birthday. _____ (open/presents)
3 We can't wait for the soloist any longer. _____ (start/concert)

Construction B

It's time (about time, high time) + agent + past tense (subjunctive) = I think the time has come.

Examples:
It's time *she went* home.
It's high time *she left.*
Don't you think it's about time *your students started* thinking about the exam?

 Exercise 38

Write sentences using 'it's time + person + past' from the following:

1 It's ten o'clock already and your wife will be expecting you home. _____ (you/leave)
2 My car is filthy, and it's my job to wash it. _____ (I/wash)
3 Your hair is far too long _____ (have/cut). [See page 87.]

 Exercise 39

Complete each of the following sentences in such a way that it has the same meaning as the sentence before it.

1 It's time for us to go.
   It's time we ____left____.

2 It's time they locked the doors.
   It's time for _____.

3 I really think we should buy a new car.
   I really think it's time we _____.

4 You must stop writing at once.
   It's time you ___stopped writing___. [Is it necessary to repeat 'at once'?]

5 Mr White, you know you ought to give up smoking, or at least smoke fewer cigarettes.
   Mr White, you know it's time you ___gave up smoking___ / ___cut down___.

6 We can't wait. You must give the signal now.
   We can't wait. It's time for ___us to leave___.

7 The people in charge ought to take their responsibilities more seriously.
   It's time the people in charge ___took their___ ___—___

△ *Note:* Passive constructions are also possible with both constructions A and B.

Examples:
It's time *for the bell to be rung/the bell was rung.*
It's time *the doors were opened/for the doors to be opened.*

Concealed relatives

In some kinds of relative sentences the relative words 'who', 'which', 'that' can be omitted.

Examples:
This is the new hat I have just bought. (... the new hat *which* I have just bought)
That's the girl I danced with all last night. (the girl *with whom* I danced ...)

Notice that prepositions are placed at the end of the relative construction. (the girl I danced *with*)

 Exercise 40

Complete each of the following sentences, using a 'concealed relative' construction where possible, in such a way that it has a similar meaning to the sentence above.

Example:
The police were looking for a man with a broken nose.
The man _____.

Answer: The man the police were looking for had a broken nose.

1. I drink in that pub.
   That's the _____.
2. He stole a car; where is it?
   Where is _____?
3. My friend belongs to an expensive golf club.
   The golf club _____.
4. When the teacher asks questions, Ray answers them all.
   Ray answers all _____.
5. I love the girl you are speaking about.
   You are _____.
6. I hate this kind of weather.
   This is _____.
7. Which window did he fall out of?
   Which is _____?
8. I live in a village which has only sixty inhabitants.
   The village I _____.
9. We stayed at a hotel on the sea-front.
   The hotel where _____.
10. Here's the room I live in.
    Here's the room where _____.

Must not/needn't/don't have to

Construction A

You *must not* do that.
You *are not allowed to* do that. } = It is against the rules
You *are forbidden to* do that.

Example:
It is against the rules to park your car here.
You _____.

Answer: You *are not allowed* to park your car here.

Construction B

We *needn't* do that.
We *don't need to* do that. } = it is not necessary
We *don't have to* do that.

We *didn't need to* do that. } it was not necessary
We *didn't have to* do that. = (so we probably did not do it)

Example 1:
It is not necessary to pay if you don't want to.
You don't _____.

Answer: You *don't need* to pay if you don't want to.

Example 2:
Yesterday was a holiday. There was no need to go to school.
We _____.

Answer: We *didn't have* to go to school yesterday.

Construction C

We *needn't have done* that. = We did it, although it was not necessary.

Example:
We paid the money, but in fact there was no obligation to do so.
We needn't _____.

Answer: We *needn't have* paid the money.

 Exercise 41

Complete each of the following sentences in such a way that it has the same meaning as the sentence before it.

1 Don't do that unless you want to.
   You _____.
2 Your visit here yesterday was quite unnecessary.
   You _____.
3 I didn't buy a ticket, because I knew it was not necessary.
   I didn't buy a ticket, because I knew I _____.
4 It is against the rules for you to have visitors in your room.
   You _____.
5 Students are forbidden to park in front of the school.
   Students are not _____.
6 It was unnecessary for Peter to go to the match, but he went.
   Peter _____.
7 Feeding the animals is forbidden.
   You _____.
8 I'm glad to see you, but actually there was no need for you to come.
   I'm glad to see you, but actually you _____.

For/since/ago

Examples:
I haven't smoked *for fifteen years*.
I haven't smoked *since 1983*.
It's fifteen years *since* I { smoked.
                              have smoked.
I stopped smoking *fifteen years ago*.

 Exercise 42

Make the following notes into complete sentences using 'for' with the present perfect tense.

Example:
I/not smoke/fifteen years.
I *haven't* smoked *for* fifteen years.

1 She/not visit us/a long time.
2 I/live in France/ten years.
3 Mr and Mrs Harrison/not go to the cinema/ages.
4 You/not wash up/six months.
5 I/teach/years.

 Exercise 43

Make the following notes into complete sentences using 'since'.

Example:
Fifteen years/I work
It's fifteen years *since* I worked/have worked.

1 Twelve years/I live in London.
2 She/not drive/her accident.
3 They/dance/six o'clock this evening.
4 Ages/I see Paul.
5 Months/I play tennis.

 Exercise 44

Complete the following sentences using 'ago'.

Example:
I haven't played volley ball for fifteen years.
I stopped _____.

Answer: I stopped playing volleyball fifteen years *ago*.

1 She hasn't had a holiday since 1978, and it's now 1988.
   She last _had_ a holiday ten years ago.
2 I haven't done any work in the garden for three months.
   The last time I did any work in the garden _was_ three months ago.
3 The man has been a priest for twelve years.
   He became _a priest twelve years ago, 1988_
4 My neighbours have lived in their house since 1945, and it is now 1988.
   My neighbours bought _their house 43 years ago_
5 I haven't had a cold for two years!
   I last _had a_ cold two years ago

Exercise 45

Complete each of the following sentences, using either 'for', 'since' or 'ago', in such a way that it has a similar meaning to the sentence above.

Example:
He began to work at the school two and a half years ago.
He has worked _____.

Answer: He has worked at the school *for* two and a half years.

1. I haven't seen my cousin for ages.
   It's ages *since* I saw my cousin

2. The last time we visited the seaside was ten years ago.
   We haven't _____.

3. He has been a politician for twenty years.
   He became _____.

4. It's many years since we've had a really hot summer.
   We haven't *had a really hot summer for many years*

5. I last went sailing at Christmas.
   I haven't *sailed since christmas*

Still/yet

Still and yet have similar meanings, but are *used* quite differently. Look very carefully at the examples below to see some of their different uses.

Still: He began his book ten years ago and he is *still* writing it.
When she arrived to take him out, he was *still* getting ready.
Is the room free, or is he *still* there?
We waited for an hour, but then, as they *still* hadn't arrived, we went home.

Yet: You can't go in there – he hasn't finished *yet*.
I'm afraid we can't start the lecture on time – the lecturer isn't here *yet*.
Have you done your homework *yet*?

Exercise 46

Complete each of the following sentences, using either 'still' or 'yet', in such a way that it has a similar meaning to the sentence above.

Example:
The house is still unsold.
Nobody has _____.

Answer: Nobody has bought the house yet.

1. I still haven't met Dr Murphy.
   I haven't _____.

2. He's still in the house.
   He hasn't *come out yet*

3. Haven't you finished making that dress yet?
   Are you *still making them?*

4. I hadn't completed my homework when he arrived.
   I was _____.

5. I don't think he has finished his meal yet.
   I think he is *still eating his meal*

Noun or verb

Many common words can be used both as nouns and verbs (examples: look, smell, touch, feel, squeeze, stroke, kiss, lick, bite, shout, scream, glance, frown, stare, peep, snore, kick, wash, rest, walk, drive, run, laugh, etc.)

Examples:
She gave me a *kiss*.
She *kissed* me.

He *glanced* at me quickly.
He gave me a quick *glance*.

I should like *to walk* for a long way.
I should like to go for a long *walk*.

△ *Note:* Adverbs go with verbs; adjectives go with nouns (see second example above).

Exercise 47

Complete each of the following sentences in such a way that it has the same meaning as the sentence before it.

1. He gave a loud scream when he saw the mouse.
   He screamed _____.

2. I kicked the ball violently.
   I gave *the ball violent kick*

3. She gave my arm an affectionate squeeze.
   She squeezed _____

4. He washed his hands and face quickly.
   He gave *his hands and face quick wash*

5. I feel like resting for a long time.
   I feel like a *long rest*

So do I/I do too/nor can I/neither can I/I can't either

Examples:

Virginia is beautiful.
{ *So is* Ruth.
  Ruth is, *too*. }

Norman isn't very clever.
{ *Nor is* Reggie.
  Neither is Reggie.
  Reggie isn't, *either*. }

 Exercise 48

Complete each of the following sentences in such a way that it has the same meaning as the sentence before it.

1 I can't swim. Nor can Simon.
   I can't swim. Simon _____.

2 I hate fish. So do they.
   I hate fish. They _____.

3 They haven't got much money. We haven't, either.
   They haven't got much money. Neither _____.

4 John loves his work. Mick does, too.
   John loves his work. So _____.

5 I don't go out very much. Carolyn doesn't, either.
   I don't go out very much. Nor *does Carolyn*.

Comparison

It may be necessary for you to use your grammar books to remind yourself of the different ways of making comparisons with adjectives and adverbs.

Below are some examples of comparisons that may be tested by means of 'conversion' exercises. Notice particularly the way in which various negative and positive constructions can be used to produce sentences with similar meanings.

Examples:
The fault in the engine is *much more serious* this time *than* it was the last time.
The fault in the engine was *not as serious* last time *as* it is this time.

People are *much less friendly* nowadays *than* they were.
People are *not as friendly* nowadays *as* they were.

John is *easier* to understand *than* Phil (is).
Phil is *not as easy* to understand *as* John (is).

She *cooks better than* I do.
I *don't cook as well* as she does.

We used to *work more hours than* we do now.
We *don't work as many hours as* we used to.

 Exercise 49

Example:
Tony drinks six cups of tea a day.
Elizabeth drinks ten cups of tea a day.

Elizabeth *drinks more cups of tea a day than* Tony (does).
Tony *does not drink as many cups of tea a day as* Elizabeth (does).
or
Tony *does not drink as much tea as* Elizabeth (does).

Using the patterns shown above, write two sentences, one 'positive' and one 'negative' for each of the following:

1 John is 1.80 m tall.
   Peter is 1.75 m tall.

2 My examination result was 90 per cent.
   My sister's examination result was 50 per cent.

3 Petrol in England costs 39p a litre.
   Petrol in Spain costs 43p a litre.

4 The plant grew 50 cms last year.
   The plant grew 30 cms this year.

5 She used to weigh 55 kg.
   She now weighs 50 kg.

PAPER 3

Exercise 50

Complete the second sentence in each of the following pairs of sentences so that it means the same as the first sentence.

1. She plays tennis better than I do.
   I don't _____.
2. People do not have as many children as they used to.
   People used to _____.
3. Beethoven's Seventh Symphony is not as long as his Ninth.
   Beethoven's Ninth Symphony _____.
4. Tennis is more exciting than squash.
   Squash is not _____.
5. The TV doesn't work as well as it used to.
   The TV used to _____.
6. The water's colder than it was.
   The water's not _____.
7. Paul is more intelligent than his brother John.
   John is _____.

Comparative/superlative

The comparative can be used to test the superlative.

Example:
There is *no* mountain in the world that is *higher* than Mount Everest.
Mount Everest is the *highest* mountain in the world.

(Notice the change from a negative form to a positive form in the above example.)

Exercise 51

Complete each of the following sentences in such a way that it has the same meaning as the sentence before it.

1. I was happier than ever before on the day I passed my entrance examination.
   The day I passed my entrance examination was _____.
2. I had never seen a more beautiful view.
   The view was _____.
3. There is no experience which is more exciting than ski-ing fast down a mountain.
   Ski-ing fast down a mountain is _____.

So ... that
Such (a) ... that
Too ... (for ...) to ...
Not ... enough to ...

The pieces of information given in the three sentences below can be combined in different ways, using constructions that are often tested by means of 'conversion' exercises.

Example:
The table was very heavy. He could not lift it.
He was not strong.

a) The table was *so heavy that* he could not lift it.
b) It was *such a heavy table* that he could not lift it.
c) The table was *too heavy for him to lift*.
d) He was *not strong enough to* lift the heavy table.

Look carefully at the further examples below to see how each of the constructions is formed.

So ... that

- My car is *so* slow *that* everybody overtakes me. (so + adjective)
- He ran *so* quickly *that* nobody could catch him. (so + adverb)
- There were *so* many people at the match *that* I could not see anything. (so + many/much/ little/few + noun)

Such ... that

- It was *such* a warm day *that* all the men were in shirt-sleeves. (such + a [+ adjective] + countable noun)
- They are *such* stupid people *that* I refuse to speak to them again. (such [+ adjective] + plural countable noun)
- It was *such* cold weather *that* even the penguins froze in their pond. (such [+ adjective] + uncountable noun)

Too ... to

- The information was far *too* complicated for the computer *to* handle. (too + adjective [+ for + agent] + to)
- He spoke *too* quickly for anybody *to* understand. (too + adverb [+ for + agent] + to)

100

Not . . . enough to

- I am *not* well *enough to* go to work yet.
  (not + adjective + enough + to)
- We had*n't enough* money *to* buy the car.
  (not + enough + noun + to)

 Exercise 52

Look back to the examples at the beginning of this section to remind yourself of the four constructions. Use each of these four constructions in turn to express different combinations of the information given in each of the five situations below. Remember that it is not necessary to include all the information in each sentence.

1 The question was very difficult. He could not answer it. He was not very clever.
2 The door handle was very high. The child could not reach it. He was not very tall.
3 The gap was very narrow. He could not squeeze through it. He was rather fat.

4 The radio message was very faint. I could not hear it clearly. My equipment was not very powerful.
5 He was still a young boy. He could not join the navy.

 Exercise 53

Complete each of the following sentences in such a way that it has a similar meaning to the one before it. (In this, as in many conversion exercises, a change in one part of a sentence makes other changes automatically necessary: see previous pages for examples of additional changes that may be needed and for further practice of these points.)

Example 1:
He walked so slowly that we got tired of waiting for him.
He was such _____.
Answer: He was such a slow walker that we got tired of waiting for him.

Example 2:
It was such a foggy night that everyone stayed inside.
It was too _____.
Answer: It was too foggy (for anyone) to go out.

1 The map was so old that I couldn't read it.
   It was such _____.
2 The weather was too cold for anyone to go out.
   It was such _____.
3 The writing was not big enough for us to read.
   The writing was so _____.
4 It was such terrible news that nobody believed it.
   The news was too terrible _____.
5 The team played too badly to win the championship.
   The team did not play _____.
   The team played so _____.
6 The scenery was so beautiful that it took my breath away.
   It was such _____.
7 There were so few people present that the concert could not take place.
   The audience was so _____.
   There were not _____.
8 They were such tiring exercises that I couldn't do them.
   The exercises were too _____.
9 He was so far ahead that we could not see him.
   He was such _____.
10 They are so inhospitable that they never invite people into their home.
    They are such _____.

'Uncountables'

'Uncountable' nouns are those which only have a singular form, and therefore cannot be used with 'a', 'many', or 'a few'. The following are some 'uncountables' which frequently cause problems for learners of English:

information	accommodation
news	knowledge
luggage	progress
advice	scenery
furniture	experience (= knowledge or skill
weather	gained by doing or seeing things)

 Exercise 54

This exercise practises not only 'uncountables' but several other conversion points, e.g. 'concealed' relatives, so/such, passives, etc.

Example:
I heard some very bad news.
The news _____.

Answer: The news *I heard was* very bad.

1 I received some excellent advice from my father.
   The advice _____.

2 Somebody has stolen my luggage.
   My luggage _____.

3 We saw some beautiful scenery.
   The scenery _____.

4 We went out because the weather was so beautiful.
   It was such _____.

5 A lot of furniture is not necessary in this room.
   We don't need _____.

6 Not much information is available.
   Very _____.

7 We have made very little progress.
   Not _____.

Adverbs/adjectives

Example 1:
She drives *recklessly*.
She is _____.

Answer: She is a *reckless* driver.

Example 2:
He was an *entertaining* writer.
He wrote _____.

Answer: He wrote *entertainingly*.

△ *Note:*
1 Adverbs with irregular forms: 'hard', 'fast', 'late' (note the special meanings of hardly, lately)
2 Verbs of 'appearance' take adjectives, not adverbs ('look', 'sound', 'smell', 'feel', 'seem', 'appear')

Examples:
She seems *nice*.
That smells *good*.
He appears *tired*.
You look *wonderful*.

But 'look', 'smell', 'taste', 'feel', 'appear' must be used with adverbs when expressing their meanings other than 'appear'.

Examples:
He tasted the hot soup *cautiously*.
The doctor *gently* felt my arm.
He *suddenly* appeared at the door.

Compare: The man looked *suspicious*:
             The policeman looked at him *suspiciously*.

             The liquid smelt *revolting*:
             I smelt it *cautiously*.

Exercise 55

Complete the second sentence in each of the following pairs of sentences so that it means the same as the first sentence.

Example 1:
He drives *very slowly*.
He is _____.

Answer: He is a *very slow* driver.

Example 2:
She had a rather *peculiar* feeling.
She felt _____.

Answer: She felt rather *peculiar*.

1 There's a funny smell in the cellar.
   The cellar _____.

2 She gave me a mysterious look.
   She looked _____.

3 That house has an extremely odd look about it.
   That house looks _____.

4 He's a very quick speaker.
   He speaks _____.

5 He climbs rather carelessly.
   He is _____.

6 His appearance at the door was very sudden.
   He _____.

7 This beer has an extremely unpleasant taste!
   This beer tastes _____.

Prefer/would rather/would prefer

Comparison: which of two you prefer

Examples:
I *prefer* lychees to kumquats.
I *prefer* walking to running.
I'd (= would) *rather* work than sleep.
I'd (= would) *prefer* to live by the sea rather than live in the town.

Exercise 56

Complete each of the following sentences in such a way that it has the same meaning as the sentence before it.

1 'I would much rather listen to people than talk to them.'
   She said she preferred _____.

2 'I prefer watching TV to listening to the radio.'
   He claimed that he'd rather _____.

3 We would prefer to live in Australia rather than in England.
   We would definitely rather _____.

Expressing what you want to do or what you want someone else to do

Examples:
'Why not come back for some coffee?' 'I'd *rather* go home, if you don't mind.'
'Come up and see my stamp collection.' 'Actually, I'd *prefer* to have another coffee.'
'I'd *prefer you* not to punch Charles's head, Diana!'
'I'd *rather you* didn't ask me about the holiday, please.'
(always past tense form after 'I'd rather you . . .')
'I think Charles *would rather you* went round to the back door with the coal.'

Exercise 57

Complete each of the following sentences in such a way that it has the same meaning as the sentence before it.

1 'How about a drink?' 'I'd prefer something to eat.'
   'How about a drink?' 'I'd rather _____.'

2 'I'd rather not go out tonight.'
   'I'd prefer _____.'

3 'I'd prefer you not to talk to me like that.'
   'I'd rather you _____.'

Miscellaneous

Here is a selection of other structures which can effectively be tested by the 'conversion exercise' technique. In each case look at the example given, then try to make a similar conversion.

What (a) + adjective

Example 1:
The news is terrible!
What _____!

Answer: What terrible news!

Example 2:
You have very beautiful children.
What _____!

Answer: What beautiful children you have!

△ *Note:* Countable nouns have 'a'; uncountables and plurals have no 'a'.

Exercise 58

1 The weather is lovely today.
   What _____!

2 That's a beautiful garden.
   What _____!

3 She has lovely eyes.
   What _____!

Pay/cost

Example:
How much did that coat cost?
How much did you _____?

Answer: How much did you *pay for* that coat?

Exercise 59

1. I don't want our new car to cost more than £5,000.
   I don't want us _____.
2. He paid a lot of money for his house.
   His house _____.

It took me/I spent

Example:
It took me three weeks to read War and Peace.
I spent _____.

Answer: I spent three weeks reading War and Peace.

Exercise 60

1. Every day I spend two hours travelling to work.
   It takes me _____.
2. It took Mr Humphries half an hour to find a taxi.
   Mr Humphries spent _____.

It takes (five hours) to get to/it's a (five-hour) journey to

Example:
It's a five-hour journey to Aberdeen.
It takes _____.

Answer: It takes (you) five hours to get to Aberdeen.

Exercise 61

1. The journey will probably take two days.
   It'll probably be *two days' journey*.
2. It's a twenty-minute drive from my home to the office.
   It takes me *twenty-min to drive*

You'd better/if I were you

Example:
You'd better go to bed early tonight.
If I were you, _____.

Answer: If I were you, I'd go to bed early tonight.

Exercise 62

1. You'd better not go out tonight.
   If I were you, _____.
2. If I were you, I'd say 'no'.
   You'd better *say 'no'*.

Why didn't I/I should have

Example:
Oh dear! Why didn't I work last night?
I should have _____.

Answer: I should have worked last night.

Exercise 63

1. It was a really good party. Why didn't you come?
   It was a really good party. You _____.
2. He should have remembered his wife's birthday.
   Why _____?

Think/mistake for

Example:
I thought it was an elephant.
I mistook _____.

Answer: I mistook it for an elephant.

Exercise 64

1. I'm sorry! I thought you were my wife!
   I'm sorry! I mistook _____!
2. She mistook the new teacher for a student.
   She thought _____.

Gerund/infinitive

Example:
It is boring to stay at home all day.
Staying _____.

Answer: Staying at home all day is boring.

Exercise 65

1. Watching a big football match is exciting.
   It _____.
2. It is very frightening to think about some of the world's present problems.
   Thinking _____.

It/there

Example 1:
The table was in the middle of the room.
There _____.

Answer: There was a table in the middle of the room.

Example 2:
My bucket has got a hole in it.
There _____.

Answer: There's a hole in my bucket.

Example 3:
It is pointless doing that.
There's _____.

Answer: There's no point doing that.

Example 4:
There's no possibility of doing that.
It _____.

Answer: It is not possible to do that.

Exercise 66

1 Some men were running down the road behind her.
  There _____.
2 That question has no answer.
  There _____.

The only/except

Example 1:
The only thing he hadn't done was lock the door.
He'd done _____.

Answer: He'd done everything *except* lock the door.

Example 2:
I know everyone in my village except my next-door neighbour.
The only _____.

Answer: *The only* person in my village that I don't know is my next-door neighbour.

Exercise 67

1 They took everything except the kitchen sink on holiday.
  The only thing they _____.
2 The only place I won't visit next year is Outer Mongolia.
  I'll visit _everywhere except ~~visiting~~ Outer Mongolia_

Any/some/no-/one/thing/where/body

Example 1:
There wasn't anybody in the room.
There was _____.

Answer: There was *nobody* in the room.

Example 2:
Nothing will stand in my way.
There isn't _____.

Answer: There *isn't anything* that will stand in my way.

Example 3:
There is nowhere in the world that I haven't visited.
There isn't _____.

Answer: There *isn't anywhere* in the world that I haven't visited.

Exercise 68

1 I know nobody who would do it better.
  I don't _anybody who would do it better_
2 Nothing is too much trouble for him.
  There isn't _anything that is too much trouble for him_
3 There isn't anyone living on the island now.
  There is _one living on the island now_ / _no_

I'm sure he hasn't/he can't have

Example:
I'm sure he hasn't gone out.
He can't _____.

Answer: He can't have gone out.

Exercise 69

1 I'm sure I haven't met you before.
  I can't _have met you before_
2 They can't have seen the house before.
  I'm sure _I haven't seen the house before_

Not as many/much as ... more than

Example 1:
There were not as many people in church this week as last week.
There were _____.

Answer: There were *more* people in church last week *than* this week.

Example 2:
More food is wasted in America than in India.
Not _____.

Answer: *Not as* much food is wasted in India *as in* America.

Exercise 70

1. More money is spent on defence than on education.
   Not _____.
2. More people live in Tokyo than in London.
   Not _____.
3. There is not as much leisure time nowadays as there used to be.
   There used to be _more leisure time than nowadays_.
4. Not as many people go to the cinema nowadays.
   More people _used to go to the cinema than nowadays._

Little few — many/much

'not much' means '(very) little'
'not many' means '(very) few'

Example 1:
Not much news has come out of Amphibia recently.
Very _____.

Answer: Very *little* news has come out of Amphibia recently.

Example 2:
There are very few people I'd trust with my money.
There are not _____.

Answer: There are *not many* people I'd trust with my money.

Exercise 71

1. Very little information has been received in the last few months.
   Not _very much information has been_
2. There are not many chairs in this room.
   There are very _few chairs in this room_

Many/few — small/large

Example:
There were so few students in the class that I cancelled the lesson.
The class was _____.

Answer: The class was *so small* that I cancelled the lesson.

Exercise 72

1. There were so many absentees in the team that the match had to be postponed.
   The team was so _small_.
2. The audience was so large that it spread out of the hall and into the street.
   There were _so many people in the audience that_

Had to wait/keep (us) waiting

Example:
We had to wait for two hours before he finally arrived.
He kept _____.

Answer: He *kept us waiting* for two hours before he finally arrived.

Exercise 73

1. The factory kept me waiting six months for my new car.
   I had _____.
2. She'll have to wait for ages for her boyfriend because he's in the middle of a tennis match.
   Her boyfriend will _____.

Not very far/a long way — quite near/so far

Example 1:
It's not far to the city centre from here.
The city centre is quite _____.

Answer: The city centre is *quite near* here.

Example 2:
It was such a long way that we decided to take a taxi.
It was so _____.

Answer: It was *so far* that we decided to take a taxi.

Exercise 74

1. My office is not far from my home.
   I live quite _near my office_.
2. It's so far that I think I'll go by train.
   It's such _a long way that I think I'll go by train_
3. It's only a short distance from here to my house.
   My house is not _very far from here_

USE OF ENGLISH

Not very often — rarely/hardly ever/seldom

Example:
He rarely visits his old mother nowadays.
He doesn't _____.

Answer: He doesn't visit his old mother *very often* nowadays. ~~hardly ever~~

Exercise 75

1 People seldom catch fish in this lake.
  People don't _catch fish — very often_.
2 When I lived abroad I didn't speak English very often.
  When I lived abroad I hardly _ever spoke English_

I don't think/I doubt

Example:
I don't think I'll go on Sunday.
I doubt _____.

Answer: I doubt *if/whether* I'll go on Sunday.

Exercise 76

1 He doubted if they would ever succeed.
  He didn't _think_.
2 Nobody thought he would ever master the piano.
  People doubted _if he would_
3 She doesn't think the painting will sell.
  She doubts _it_.

Can't go/prevent from

Example:
We couldn't go because of the weather.
The weather _____.

Answer: The weather *prevented us from* going.

Exercise 77

1 Her sore throat prevented her from singing.
  She couldn't _____.
2 The plane couldn't take off because of bad visibility.
  Bad visibility prevented _____.

(Only) when/until

Example:
We only dig the garden when the good weather has arrived.
We wait until _____.

Answer: We wait *until* the good weather has arrived before we dig the garden.

Exercise 78

1 We started doing the washing up when the guests had gone.
  We waited until _____.
2 She waited until the storm had finished before she set off for the hills.
  She set off for the hills _when the storm had finished_

3 Changing the form of words in context

In this type of question you are asked to look at a word in CAPITALS at the end of a sentence and to change the form of the word so that it fits suitably into the blank space.

Example:
He said 'Good morning' in a most _____ way.
FRIEND
Answer: friendly

In order to attempt this question you have first to identify the 'function' of the required word:

- Is it a concrete noun? (friend)
- Is it an abstract noun? (friendship)
- Is it a positive adjective? (successful) or a negative one? (unsuccessful)
- Is it a positive adverb? (successfully) or a negative one? (unsuccessfully)
- Is it a positive verb? (encourage) or a negative one? (discourage)
- Is it singular or plural? (country/countries)

Secondly, having identified the 'function', you must put the correct form of the word into the sentence. To do this exercise well, you need a good knowledge of English nouns, verbs, adjectives and adverbs. Below is one suggested way of increasing this knowledge.

Do-it-yourself word-building

From time to time, take one or two sentences from your own reading, underline some of the nouns, verbs and adjectives, look in your dictionary for other forms of the word and write them down in table form in a notebook.

Example 1:
It is *true* to say that in the *history* of *art*, Italian *painting* has been of prime *importance*.

Concrete Noun*	Abstract Noun	Verb	Adjective ±
	truth		(un)true
historian	history		(un)truthful
			historic
			historical
artist	art		(in)artistic
(a) painting	painting	to paint	painted
painter			
	importance		(un)important

Example 2:
It was *strange travelling* by air for the first time, but I was *comforted* by an *extremely* pretty stewardess with *deep* brown eyes.

Concrete Noun*	Abstract Noun	Verb	Adjective ±
stranger	strangeness		strange
traveller	travel	to travel	travelling
	(dis)comfort	to comfort	(un)comfortable
extremist	extreme		extreme
	depth	to deepen	deep

*Concrete noun is used here and in Appendix 3 (page 131) to describe people, places and things – things that you can see or touch.

We have not included a box for adverbs, either here or in Appendix 3, for reasons of space. With a very few exceptions (e.g. well, hard, fast, late), adverbs in English are formed by adding -ly to the adjective form. This sometimes involves a spelling change (happy – happily).

 Exercise 79

Now do the same with the following words printed in italics. It is not always possible to find a word for every box, so the ones you should complete have been marked _____.

1 My *advice* to *tourists* when *visiting* a *foreign* country is to *behave* normally.

Concrete Noun	Abstract Noun	Verb	Adjective ±
tourists	advice	_____	_____
_____	_____	to visit	
_____	_____		foreign
		to (mis)behave	

2 The *scientist* was *dismissed* by his *employer* for making the wrong *decision*.

Concrete Noun	Abstract Noun	Verb	Adjective ±
scientist	_____		_____
	_____	to dismiss	
employer	_____		_____
	decision		_____

3 The *dangerous criminal* escaped over the *high* wall by building a flying *machine*.

Concrete Noun	Abstract Noun	Verb	Adjective ±
criminal	_____		dangerous
	_____		_____
machine	_____	_____	high
	_____		

Take a sentence from your own reading from time to time, and deal with it in the same way.

Important

Word-building is not the same as word-collecting. Words cannot be 'learnt' until you know how to *use* them correctly, and it is most important to practise using the words you find by writing them in correct English sentences. Translation into your own language can be misleading, as words may be used in quite different ways in different languages.

The aim of the previous activity was to build on to the knowledge you already had. For example, you probably knew the word 'comfortable', but did you know the words 'comfort' and 'discomfort'?

You will have to use your dictionary carefully and selectively. It is important not to collect *every* derivative of a word, but only to write down those words which are likely to be useful. Concentrate on finding *common* nouns, verbs, adjectives, and negative forms. If possible check with your teacher or a native English speaker that the words you have chosen are ones which are frequently used.

For further study

Appendix 3 gives you a ready-made list of common words: remembering what we have said above, study these and use them, in conjunction with your English-English dictionary and its examples of correct usage, to improve your performance in this question.

If you have any difficulty with the following practice exercise, look at Appendix 3 for reference and see if you can find the appropriate word.

Exercise 80

The word in capitals at the end of each of the following sentences can be used to form a word that fits suitably in the blank space. Fill each blank in this way.

Example:
If you want to be away from school next week you will have to ask the headmistress's _____. PERMIT

Answer: permission

1 Everybody found the talk _____: five people even fell asleep. BORE
2 It is time a _____ was made about the new school. DECIDE
3 Number 10 Shaftesbury Avenue was burnt down last night and the Thatcher family are now _____. HOME
4 How do you manage to be such an _____ person? ENERGY
5 Many people say that _____ is the happiest time of your life. CHILD
6 I am not _____ in my job. INTEREST
7 It rained all day and they were wet through. In fact, it was a very _____ day. PLEASE
8 All _____ should be given, in writing, to the secretary. COMPLAIN
9 The cinema or the theatre tonight? You decide, it's your _____. CHOOSE
10 As a young boy, one of my hobbies was _____ stamps. COLLECT
11 We live in a lovely _____ where all the people know and help each other. NEIGHBOUR
12 A. J. Sailor, the famous _____, came to London to give a lecture last week. HISTORY
13 I'm sorry, sir. If you haven't made a _____ I'm afraid we can't take you. RESERVE
14 She never regrets marrying him, and she has now been _____ married for twenty years. HAPPY
15 If the strike isn't settled soon there'll be a _____ of bread. SHORT

4 Guided sentence writing

The information in this type of exercise is presented in 'skeleton' form and the aim is to produce grammatically correct sentences which together make a complete passage (usually a letter).

You produce a sentence (a) by adding words, and (b) by changing the verbs where necessary.

Example:
It/be/kind/you/remember/my birthday.
It *was*
It *is* } kind *of* you *to* remember my birthday.

Points to remember

1 Read through the whole passage first and decide whether, in general, it is past, present or future.

2 Pay particular attention to places where 'little' words like prepositions, pronouns, articles, etc. may be needed to complete the sense:

Example:
Thank/you/very much/present/just/arrive.
Thank you very much
for { *the*
your } present, *which* has just arrived.

3 As this exercise is very often presented in the form of a letter, be prepared for changes in the verb tenses:

Examples:
Thank you/your letter/I receive/yesterday.
Thank you very much for your letter which I *received* yesterday.

At the moment/I study English/school/in Worcester and after Christmas/I join/my sister/university.
At the moment I *am studying* English at a school in Worcester and after Christmas I'*m going to* join my sister *at* university.

4 Read through the whole passage when you have finished to make sure the sentences have a clear and logical meaning.

5 Look back to page 59 to remind yourself of the phrases used in letters, particularly at the beginning and end.

 Exercise 81

Make all the changes and additions necessary to produce, from the following six series of words and phrases, six correct sentences which together make a complete letter.

Dear Uncle Mark,

1 It/be/lovely/see/you/Friday and/hear/latest news.
2 Your trip/Amazon basin/sound/be/terribly exciting;/I/wish/I/lead/such/adventurous life/you.
3 Be there/chance/I come with you/next trip?
4 I/be free/as soon as I/finish the job/I do/at present.
5 Of course if you/rather/I not come/I/quite understand.
6 But I/love/variety, and I/love/go with you,/so let me know.

Best wishes,
Steve

 Exercise 82

Do the same with this letter:

Dear Julia,

1 What/lovely surprise/get your letter.
2 I/feel very lonely/recently/and your letter/cheer me up.
3 I/happy/know/you/come/to France/next month.
4 Not forget/tell me/exact time of arrival/so I meet/you/at airport.
5 Weather be/warm/next month/I think. If it be/we go/the south coast/sunbathe.
6 Look forward/see you/soon.
7 Give/my best wishes/your parents.

With love,
Shaun

5 Incomplete dialogues

In this kind of question you must fill in the missing sections in the sentences of a dialogue. What you write must be grammatically correct, and must make sense in the context of the whole conversation. You will need to pay particular attention to verb tenses, question forms and negatives.

Example:
CAROLYN: Well, Rose, what (1) _____ this evening?
ROSE: (2) _____ cinema?
CAROLYN: No, I (3) _____ twice already this week: I (4) _____ again!

Answer:
CAROLYN: Well, Rose, what *would you like to do* this evening?
ROSE: *Shall we go to the* cinema?
CAROLYN: No, *I've been* twice already this week: I *don't want to go* again!

or

CAROLYN: Well, Rose, what *do you fancy doing* this evening?
ROSE: *How about going* to the cinema?
CAROLYN: No, *I've been* twice already this week: I *don't feel like going* again!

Points to remember

1 Read the whole dialogue or passage before you try to answer.
2 Look carefully at the punctuation, particularly where there are question marks.
3 Make sure that your completed sentence fits with the information given before and *after*.

 Exercise 83

Complete the sentences suitably.

JACKIE: That's settled then, we (1) _____ Spain for our holidays this summer.
MAGGIE: Good. Now, (2) _____ stay?
JACKIE: (3) _____ same place as last year, couldn't we?
MAGGIE: (4) _____.
JACKIE: Well, where do *you* suggest, then? Remember I (5) _____ much money.
MAGGIE: (6) _____ camping.
JACKIE: That's a good idea. I (7) _____ before so it'll be a new experience for me.
MAGGIE: (8) _____ by car?
JACKIE: Okay – yours or mine?
MAGGIE: I think we (9) _____; you know what mine's like!
JACKIE: How long (10) _____?
MAGGIE: About twelve hours non-stop. The only problem is (11) _____ a tent!
JACKIE: (12) _____.
MAGGIE: Good. Well, that's all organised, then.

 Exercise 84

Complete the sentences suitably.

MICK: You look tired. What (1) _____ doing?
IAN: Staying up late, working for my exams.
MICK: When (2) _____?
IAN: Next Thursday, and I'm not ready for them.
MICK: Have (3) _____ to pass?
IAN: Yes, otherwise I'll have to leave college.
MICK: I'm sure you'll be all right. You got top marks last year, (4) _____?
IAN: Yes, but that was *last* year.
MICK: Well, don't get too worried. Look, why (5) _____ to my house later for a meal?
IAN: Thanks, I'd love to. That'll take my mind off studying for a while.
MICK: Good. Oh, by the way, (6) _____ your new Randy Crawford record with you when you come?
IAN: Sure. See you later.

6 Indirect and direct speech

Another type of exercise that has appeared in this part of Paper 3 involves transferring direct speech to indirect speech, or indirect speech back to direct. In other words, you must either convert:

'Hello, Sue,' said Cathy.   into   Cathy greeted Sue.

or

Cathy greeted Sue.   into   Cathy: 'Hello, Sue.'

Direct speech to indirect speech

Look back to pages 92–4 to remind yourself of the technicalities involved here, and of some useful introductory verbs such as 'remind', 'suggest', 'refuse', etc. Then study the example below of a conversion from direct to indirect speech before attempting exercises 85 and 86.

Example:

TOM: Are you going shopping?
JACK: Yes, I am. Do you need anything from the shops?
TOM: Well, I know you're very busy.
JACK: That's all right. Why don't you just tell me what you want?
TOM: Okay, some cheese and a loaf. The trouble is I haven't got any money, I'm afraid. I can give you some tomorrow, without fail.
JACK: You'd better, or I'll be broke this weekend.

When Tom asked Jack if he was going shopping, Jack said he was and wanted to know if Tom needed anything from the shops. Tom hesitated because he knew that Jack was very busy. Jack reassured him and suggested that he should just tell him what he wanted. Tom finally agreed, and said he wanted some cheese and a loaf. He apologised that he hadn't got any money but promised he would give Jack some the following day. Jack said he hoped he would, because he would otherwise be broke that weekend.

 Exercise 85

Put the following dialogue into indirect speech, using the framework given.

TERRY: I've lost my car key. Have you seen it?
JULIAN: No, I haven't. You're always losing it.
TERRY: I'm not. I just can't remember where I put it.
JULIAN: Why don't you look in your pocket? That's where it was last time you lost it. It's about time you learnt to look after your things, you're not a child any more!
TERRY: What's the matter with you today? You're in a bad mood, aren't you?
JULIAN: Well, if you must know, I've lost *my* car key too.

Terry said that he _____ and asked if Julian _____. Julian said _____ and pointed out that _____. Terry denied this and said _____. At this point Julian suggested _____ because _____. He told Terry that _____. Terry was surprised at Julian; he asked him _____, and accused him _____. Julian admitted that _____.

Exercise 86

Put the following dialogue into indirect speech, using the information given:

POLICEMAN: How long have you known Al Capucino?
WOMAN: About two years, I think.
POLICEMAN: I want you to be more exact. Can you remember when you first met him?
WOMAN: Let me see... I was on holiday in Chicago so it must have been in October two years ago.
POLICEMAN: Good, that's what we wanted to know.
WOMAN: Is that all you want to know?
POLICEMAN: Yes, for the moment; but don't forget to let me know if you think of the address where Capucino was living when you first met him.
WOMAN: I'll do that.

Indirect speech to direct speech

In this kind of exercise, you have to *understand* what the people said to each other, and then you should try to *imagine* the actual words that they used. Again, study the example below carefully before attempting Exercise 87.

Example:
John asked Mary what she had behind her back, and she answered that she hadn't got anything. John insisted, but she still refused to show him. John wondered why not, and she replied that it was because it was a present. John hoped that it was for him and reminded her it was his birthday the following week. Mary said that it was for him, but as it wasn't his birthday yet she wasn't going to give it to him.

JOHN: What's that you've got behind your back?
MARY: Nothing.
JOHN: Come on, show me.
MARY: No, I won't!
JOHN: Why not?
MARY: Because it's a present.
JOHN: I hope it's for me. Don't forget it's my birthday next week.
MARY: It is for you, actually, but as it isn't your birthday yet I'm not going to give it to you.

Exercise 87

Put the following passage into dialogue, making all the necessary changes. The beginning has been done for you.

Cathy greeted Sue, saying it was nice to see her. Sue observed that they hadn't seen each other for a long time, and went on to say that it was about time they made an arrangement to spend an evening together. Cathy thought this was a good idea, but said that she had very little free time as the children took up most of her day. Sue told her not to worry as she often found herself with nothing to do, and she suggested that she came round to Cathy's one afternoon and took the children out. Cathy thought that that would give her time to catch up on all her jobs and then when Sue came back with the children she could stay for a meal and they could catch up on the gossip. Cathy asked if Sue really wanted to take three children out for an afternoon, but Sue assured her that she would enjoy it. They had to break off at that point since Sue had an appointment.

CATHY: Hello Sue, how nice to see you.
SUE: Hello. We haven't seen each other for ages.
_____.

7 Vocabulary and phrasal verb questions

On pages 4–6 you looked at some ways of improving your vocabulary and increasing your understanding of phrasal verbs. Paper 3 sometimes includes questions which test your knowledge in these two areas.

Vocabulary questions

Words connected with the same 'theme' may be tested. Examples from past examination papers include:

- cooking (e.g. to fry, an oven, to bake, a recipe)
- tools (e.g. a hammer, to saw, a screwdriver, a spade)
- crime (e.g. a robber, burglary, to steal)
- money (e.g. cash, discount, a loan, interest)
- 'opposites' (e.g. tighten – loosen, fresh – stale, freeze – melt, failure – success)

There is no way in which you can prepare yourself completely for this kind of question, as the examiners can test your knowledge of many hundreds of words. However, the method suggested on pages 5–6 for increasing your range of vocabulary will certainly be helpful, and you may yourself think of further 'themes' to explore.

The following exercises will not teach you much new vocabulary, but they will show you the way in which such questions may be written:

Exercise 88

Complete the following sentences with *one* appropriate word connected with *jobs* or *professions*.

Example:
When I arrived at the hotel, a _____ took my luggage up to my room.
Answer: porter

1 If your water pipes freeze and then burst, you should call a _plumber_.
2 I was served by a very polite _waiter_ in the restaurant.
3 The _judge_ sentenced the criminal to 10 years in prison.
4 It was difficult for the _fireman_ to put out the fire as the building was very old and built of wood.
5 To be successful in horse racing, a _rider/jockey_ must be careful not to put on weight.

Exercise 89

Fill each of the numbered blanks in the following passage with *one* word connected with *sport*.

Example:
After ninety minutes of exciting play, the _____ blew the whistle to end the game.
Answer: referee

St. Louis Lions *vs.* Los Angeles Angels

The 'home' crowd at the season's most important (1) _game_ cheered loudly when their best (2) _player_ scored a goal five minutes before the end; this meant that the (3) _score_ was now 8–0 and the Lions would certainly win the championship. Later, the manager of the Angels said, 'We were very disappointed that we were (4) _defeated_ so easily, but I suppose one (5) _team_ has to win.'

USE OF ENGLISH

 Exercise 90

Complete the following sentences with an appropriate word or phrase connected with *family relationships*.

Example:
Rose has just _____ _____ to the boy next door, and they plan to marry in the spring.

Answer: got engaged

1 My mother's grandfather (my _____) died only last week.
2 Janet's family is said to be distantly _____ to the Royal Family.
3 Geraldine's sister has a son and a daughter, and Geraldine always sends them Christmas presents with a little note saying, 'to my dear _____ and _____'.
4 Unfortunately their marriage was not a success, and after only three years they _____ _____, both saying that they would never remarry.
5 I have no brothers or sisters, but I have never felt lonely or regretted being a(n) _____ _____.

Phrasal verb questions

See page 4 for some notes about phrasal verbs. The following exercises are examples of how these may be tested in this part of the examination.

 Exercise 91

Complete each of the following sentences with an expression formed from the word *look*.

Example:
Don't forget to _____ _____ your work before you give it to the examiner.

Answer: look through

1 'What are you doing on the floor, Paul?' 'I'm _____ _____ my contact lenses. I've dropped them somewhere.'
2 _____ _____! There's a car coming towards us on the wrong side of the road!
3 After working hard for six months, she was really _____ _____ _____ her holiday.
4 He couldn't remember her address so he _____ it _____ in his diary.
5 She spent many years _____ _____ her elderly parents at home.

Exercise 92

Complete each of the following sentences with an expression formed from the word *run*.

Example:
The man rushed out of the jeweller's shop and the policeman _____ _____ him.

Answer: ran after

1 The car skidded and _____ _____ a lamp-post.
2 Oh dear, we've _____ _____ _____ coffee. I'll have to go and buy some more.
3 At the age of 12 she _____ _____ from school because she was unhappy.
4 The dog dashed across the road and was unfortunately _____ _____ by a passing truck.

 Exercise 93

Complete each of the following sentences with a *verb*. Write only *one* word in each sentence.

Example:
The plane for Dubai _____ off from Heathrow Airport at 10.30 a.m. yesterday.

Answer: took

1 The price of petrol is _____ up next week.
2 The bomb _____ off in the middle of a deserted car park.
3 Her children were _____ up in the country, but later moved to the city.
4 It's about time you _____ up your mind about what you want to do.
5 I'll _____ you up at 7.00 p.m., so please be ready.

8 Questions based on dialogues or texts

In this kind of exercise you must re-present selected information taken from a dialogue or text, as far as possible in your own words.

> **Sample question**
> Mrs Jackson and Mrs Skittle are discussing holidays. Mrs Jackson is going on a package holiday to North Africa. Taking your information only from their conversation, write two paragraphs of 100–200 words altogether; in the first paragraph say why a package holiday would not suit Mrs Skittle, and in the second paragraph say why Mrs Jackson likes package holidays.

MRS JACKSON: So, we're leaving Gatwick Airport at 9.00 a.m. and we'll be in North Africa at 12.00, just in time for lunch. We'll get that on the coach, of course.

MRS SKITTLE: Oh, you're having a package (5) holiday? That wouldn't suit me, I'm afraid. I'd feel too organised, like cows at a cattle market.

MRS JACKSON: It's not at all like that. It makes for convenience, you know. You don't have (10) to worry about getting meals – they're all served at the hotels. You don't have to think about what to choose or how much to tip or . . .

MRS SKITTLE: That's just my point. I like to make (15) my own decisions on holiday. Sometimes I make mistakes too, but that's all part of the fun, and you certainly remember the holiday!

MRS JACKSON: What I find really good about a (20) package tour is the fact that I know exactly how much money I'm going to spend. I mean all the excursions are included in the price. Of course, going by charter flight means a big saving. (25)

MRS SKITTLE: You don't really believe that they're good value, do you? Have you thought about the money you pay for excursions you don't go on? And as for the charter flight, well, most people these days (30) can fly cheaply without being packaged. No, it's the freedom holiday for me. Choose everything for yourself, pay only for what you want and of course you have much more opportunity to meet the real people of (35) the country.

USE OF ENGLISH

Suggested procedure

1 Read the dialogue or text very carefully at least twice.

2 Read the instructions *very* carefully. It is most important to have a clear understanding of what you are being asked to do.

3 The 'questions' you are asked about the text or dialogue will probably be in the form of 'paragraph headings' or the opening sentences of paragraphs, which you are asked to continue. When you have fully understood both the general instructions and the requirements for the *first* 'question' or 'paragraph', read through the whole text again, this time underlining *only those points which give the information you need* in order to answer the first 'question'.

4 Follow the same procedure for all the 'questions', if possible using a different coloured pen or pencil in each case.

5 Again dealing with each 'question' in turn, write down on a separate piece of paper the points you have underlined, trying to rephrase them if possible.

6 The general instructions probably contain a phrase such as 'using only the information given' or 'from the information given'. If this is the case, be careful not to introduce your own ideas.

7 Now join the points you have noted for each 'question' into connected paragraphs.

Look at the points below, taken from the conversation. Notice that the exact words of the passage are not always used. While it is not necessary or possible to find new words for every point you make, it is important that you should not simply repeat large sections of the original passage in your final answer.

Paragraph 1: Why a package holiday would not suit Mrs Skittle

- Doesn't like to feel one of crowd. (line 7)
- Likes to decide for herself. (lines 15–16)
- Even mistakes can be enjoyable and make the holiday more memorable. (lines 17–18)
- You waste money by paying for trips that you don't go on. (lines 28–9)
- Non-packaged air fares are cheap now, anyway. (line 31)
- No freedom of choice on package holidays. (same as second point above) (line 32)
- Pay for more than you want. (same as fourth point above) (lines 33–4)
- Not so much opportunity to meet the real people. (line 35)

Paragraph 2: Why Mrs Jackson likes package holidays

- Finds it very convenient. (lines 9–10)
- No worries about getting meals. (lines 10–11)
- No decisions about choosing meals. (lines 12–13)
- No problems about tipping. (lines 13–14)
- Knows how much she's going to spend – holiday price inclusive. (lines 21–4)
- Charter flight cheap. (lines 24–5)

In the two paragraphs below the points are joined together into connected sentences. Look at the words in italics, which are suggested ways of introducing and linking the points.

Sample answer
Paragraph 1
Package holidays would not suit Mrs Skittle because she hates to feel one of a crowd; she prefers to make her own decisions on holiday. She even dislikes the absence of problems on a package holiday – *she thinks* mistakes can be fun, and can make a holiday more memorable. *Another disadvantage* of the package holiday *in her opinion* is that you may waste money paying for trips that you don't go on, and *she points out* that you can fly cheaply these days without using a charter flight. *Finally*, she feels that you meet the local people less on a package holiday.

Paragraph 2
Mrs Jackson, *on the other hand*, likes package holidays because she finds them very convenient. *One advantage for her* is that she has no worries about preparing or choosing meals and *she adds that* there is no problem of how much to tip. *Mrs Jackson also points out* that with a package holiday the price is inclusive, so you know exactly how much you are going to spend. *Her final point is* that travelling by charter flight is cheap so the holiday does not cost too much.

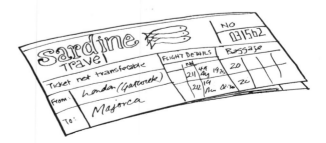

Below is a list of the introducing and linking phrases used in the sample paragraphs, together with some additional phrases. Try to use these yourself in summary exercises of this type. (Look also at pages 68–9 of the Composition section.)

- She thinks/says/mentions/finds/feels that/points out/adds that...
- In her opinion,...
- One advantage of... is...
- Another disadvantage of... is...
- On the other hand...
- Finally, she...
- Her final point is that...

The following three exercises give practice in selecting particular points from a text. In all the exercises you must decide which points really answer the question, and which are irrelevant.

Exercise 94

Look at the following paragraph about Louis XIV of France: *He could bear staying at home*

> Louis XIV was a country person. He excelled at all sport and could hardly bear to be indoors; he spent hours every day hunting or shooting. The year before his death he brought down thirty-two pheasants with thirty-four shots, a considerable feat with the primitive gun of those days. He thought nothing of riding from Fontainebleau to Paris, going to see the building in progress at the Louvre and Vincennes, dining with his brother at Saint-Cloud, inspecting the improvements there and riding back to Fontainebleau. In old age he became more and more interested in gardens. Such a man would have been miserable, cooped up in a town.
>
> From *The Sun King* by Nancy Mitford

Write down, in note-form, four points from the passage which tell you that Louis XIV was an outdoor person.

Exercise 95

Read the passage below and list in note-form the *disadvantages* of going by car.

> Going by car is one of the cheapest ways, particularly if several people travel together, despite expensive *on* petrol and the extra cost of accommodation and meals on the way. You can often save a few pounds by taking one of the short Channel ferry crossings and driving a bit further. But driving to a cheap destination like, say, Spain, can be very tiring, especially with children.
>
> From *Holiday Which?* February 1978

Exercise 96

Below the following description of Peninsula Valdes are a number of points taken from the text. Pick out only those points which give you information about *the peninsula itself*, rather than the mainland.

> Peninsula Valdes lies on the coast of the province of Chubut. It is a mass of land rather like an axe-head, some eighty miles long by thirty broad. The peninsula is almost an island, being connected to the mainland by such a narrow neck of land that, as you drive along it, you can see the sea on both sides of the road. Entering the peninsula was like coming into a new land. For days we had driven through the monotonous and monochrome Patagonian landscape, flat as a billiard-table and apparently devoid of life. Now we reached the fine neck of land on the other side of which was the peninsula, and suddenly the landscape changed. Instead of the small, spiky bushes stretching purply to the horizon, we drove into a buttercup-yellow landscape, for the bushes were larger, greener and each decked with a mass of tiny blooms. The countryside was no longer flat, but gently undulating, stretching away to the horizon like a yellow sea, shimmering in the sun.
>
> From *The Whispering Land* by Gerald Durrell

1. Landscape flat as a billiard-table.
2. Rather like an axe-head.
3. Small, spiky bushes stretching purply to the horizon.
4. On the coast of Chubut.

5 Eighty miles long by thirty broad.
6 Connected to the mainland by a very narrow neck of land.
7 Apparently devoid of life.
8 Countryside gently undulating.
9 Almost an island.
10 Monotonous and monochrome Patagonian landscape.

Exercise 97

Below is a letter about a proposed new road. List, in note-form, the reasons why the writer *does not agree* with the proposed by-pass.

Exercise 98

From your listed points in Exercise 97, write a connected paragraph saying why the writer does not agree with the proposed new by-pass. Use any phrases you can from the list of introducing and linking words on page 118.

```
                                    'Mafeking'
                                    Oxcomb
                                    Brushley
                                    Combshire
                                    29/2/88
```

Dear Sir

I am writing to protest about the proposed new road to by-pass the village of Oxcomb. The traffic through the village is, I agree, very heavy at times, but most of the houses are set well back from the road and are not much affected. The villagers themselves, and I am one of them, have not complained and indeed I know a lot of people actually welcome the traffic, as this brings life and trade to the village. We believe that a by-pass would mean a considerable financial loss among the shopkeepers and publicans in Oxcomb.

But, above all, we feel very strongly that the proposed by-pass will cut through valuable agricultural land, and will spoil an otherwise untouched part of the Combshire countryside.

Yours faithfully

J B Bright-Parsley (Colonel)

PAPER 3

9 Questions based on other source material

These can appear confusing at first sight, but essentially the exercise is the same as the last one. In other words, you must read, understand and re-present selected information. The information may be given in almost any form – a map, an advertisement, a diagram, a timetable, statistics, notes, a picture, a diary, a telegram, or any combination of these. The ways in which you may be asked to re-present the information you are given may also vary: you may have to write or complete a conversation, write a letter, continue paragraphs for which the first sentence is given, or answer a number of direct questions.

Suggested procedure

1 Read the instructions until you know exactly what is wanted.
2 Read and study all the given information slowly and carefully.
3 Use your imagination to help you understand what maps, figures, timetables, etc. really mean.
4 Be careful to select only those parts of the material that are relevant for your answer.
5 Most important: do not be in a great hurry to answer the questions until you feel ready.

Sample question

You, Mr Fatzelli, are visiting England on business and spend your first day trying to find a suitable language school in Bathport for your son, aged 18. You want him to come to England in the summer for about six weeks to improve his English before joining you in your business.

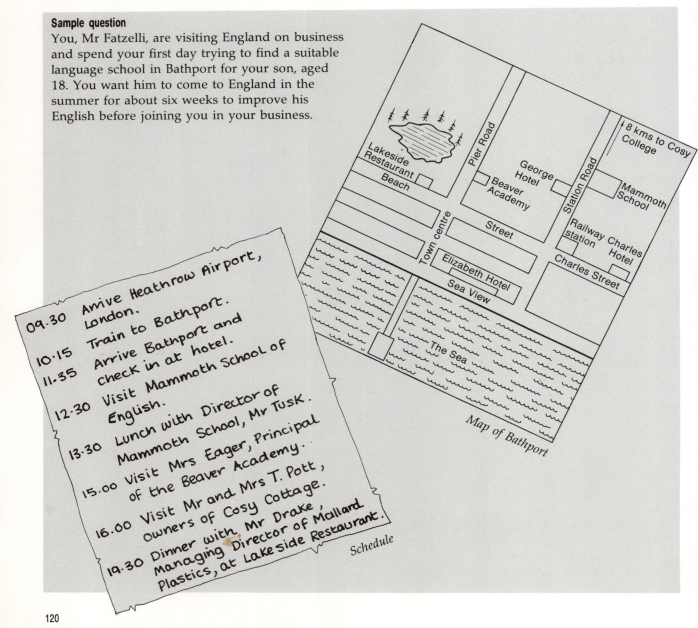

USE OF ENGLISH

Below is half of a telephone conversation between you and your secretary, Mary Flynn. It is 11.45 on the morning of your visit to Bathport, and you are telephoning from the Charles Hotel about a problem with your accommodation. With the help of the street plan and schedule opposite, write your side of the conversation.

MISS FLYNN: Mr Fatzelli's office.
MR FATZELLI: _____.
MISS FLYNN: Oh dear, what is it? Is there something wrong with the hotel?
MR FATZELLI: _____.
MISS FLYNN: That's odd. Where are you speaking from?
MR FATZELLI: _____.
MISS FLYNN: Ah well, the one I booked for you wasn't near the station; it was overlooking the sea.
MR FATZELLI: _____.
MISS FLYNN: That's right, it was the Elizabeth. I'm so sorry about the confusion.

Sample answer
MISS FLYNN: Mr Fatzelli's office.
MR FATZELLI: *Is that Mary? Look, I'm in Bathport, but there seems to be a bit of a problem.*
MISS FLYNN: Oh dear, what is it? Is there something wrong with the hotel?
MR FATZELLI: *They haven't got a reservation for me here.*
MISS FLYNN: That's odd. Where are you speaking from?
MR FATZELLI: *I'm in the Charles Hotel, just near the station.*
MISS FLYNN: Ah well, the one I booked for you wasn't near the station; it was overlooking the sea.
MR FATZELLI: *That must be the Elizabeth Hotel, then.*
MISS FLYNN: That's right, it was the Elizabeth. I'm so sorry about the confusion.

  H.W

Here are the notes that Mr Fatzelli made at each of the three schools he visited. With the help of these notes, complete Mr Fatzelli's part of the conversation with Mrs Eager of the Beaver Academy.

Mr Fatzelli's notes

Mammoth School:	length of course:	3 courses of 4 weeks
	size:	big (over 400 students)
	class size:	16 max.
	hours of study:	only mornings (9.00 a.m. to 12.00) or afternoons (2.00 p.m. to 5.00 p.m.)
	accommodation:	hostels
	facilities:	3 language laboratories, large student library.
	general impression:	good, but rather impersonal?
Beaver Academy:	length of course:	3 courses of 3 weeks
	size:	medium (120 students approx.)
	class size:	no more than 12 per class
	hours of study:	25 per week
	accommodation:	with English family
	facilities:	language laboratory, private study room
	general impression:	a serious school
Cosy College:	length of course:	2 courses of 6 weeks
	size:	small (40 students max.)
	class size:	about 10
	hours of study:	20 per week
	accommodation:	residential in the college building
	facilities:	tennis court and swimming pool
	general impression:	nice, friendly atmosphere

MR FATZELLI: *I'm looking for a school for my son to come to for six weeks in the summer.*
MRS EAGER: Well, we organise three summer courses, each lasting for three weeks, so that would fit rather well with your son's requirements.
MR FATZELLI: *You mean, he could come for two three-week courses?*
MRS EAGER: Yes, that's right.
MR FATZELLI: *Is this a big school?*
MRS EAGER: Well, we normally have about a hundred and twenty students on each course, so I wouldn't say we were too big.

(Now continue writing Mr Fatzelli's part of the conversation.)

MR FATZELLI: **(1)** _____?
MRS EAGER: They have twenty-five hours in class.
MR FATZELLI: **(2)** _____?
MRS EAGER: Oh yes, we arrange for all our students to live with English families. We think it's better.
MR FATZELLI: **(3)** _____?
MRS EAGER: We have got an up-to-date language laboratory and we have just built a private study room for the students. They can use it in their free time.
MR FATZELLI: **(4)** _____?
MRS EAGER: Twelve is the maximum number.
MR FATZELLI: **(5)** _____?
MRS EAGER: Oh yes, certainly they are. We're a very serious school. But perhaps I could ask you something about your son and why he wants to learn English?
MR FATZELLI: **(6)** _____.
MRS EAGER: Well, I hope we shall see him in the summer.

Exercise 100

In a letter to his son, Mr Fatzelli mentions various points about the schools he visited. Using all the relevant information given on page 121, continue each paragraph. You will probably need about 60 words for each paragraph. (A sample answer is given to the first paragraph.)

1 *There were some things about Cosy College that I liked and some I disliked. To begin with, it's in the middle of the countryside, which is nice, but you might feel a bit cut off from the town. They have a six-week course in the summer and the people seemed very friendly. But there aren't many students and you would live at the college, so you wouldn't really meet any other people.*

2 *The Mammoth School seemed the least suitable of the three schools,* _____.

3 *I think the best school for you this summer would definitely be the Beaver Academy.* _____.

Exercise 101

Look carefully at the train timetable on the opposite page, paying particular attention to the notes and explanations of the symbols and letters.

Now, answer the following questions in complete sentences, taking your information from the timetable; the first two questions have been answered for you:

1 How long does the Flying Scotsman take to travel from Edinburgh to London?
   It takes five and a half hours.

2 If you had an appointment in Peterborough at 6.00 p.m., what train would you catch from Dundee that morning?
   I would catch the 10.25 train.

3 Which train is the quickest from Aberdeen to London, and how long does it take?
   _____.

4 What is special about the 11.44 from Edinburgh?
   _____.

5 Why wouldn't a passenger be able to get on the train at 04.51 at Grantham?
   _____.

6 How long does it take the Night Aberdonian to reach London from Aberdeen?
   _____.

USE OF ENGLISH

Aberdeen	Dundee	Glasgow Queen Street	Edinburgh	Dunbar	Berwick-upon-Tweed	Newcastle	Darlington	York	Doncaster	Grantham	Peterborough	London King's Cross	
✕✕			07.00										
✕✕			07.00										
A	06.15		08.30										
✕✕	06.15		09.00	08.36									
✕✕	06.15		09.40		10.39							15.30	The Flying Scotsman
FO	06.15		10.00	10.34	11.05								
✕✕	07.45		10.06	11.37	12.09								
✕✕			10.00			08.54	10.29	11.19				13.40	
		07.00	08.00		09.13	10.39	11.29	12.10	12.43	13.28	14.02	15.25	
		07.00	08.05			11.42	12.36	13.18					
		08.30	09.40										
		09.00	10.00							14.52		17.28	
	07.45	09.00	10.06			11.50	12.56	13.37	15.06		16.38	17.48	
	07.45	10.00	11.10			12.06	13.50	14.33		16.35	16.45	17.55	
	08.22	10.30	11.44			13.12	14.16	14.56			18.47	20.00	The Aberdonian
	09.22	11.00	12.10			13.39	14.44	15.09	15.54				
	08.55	13.00	14.00		14.54	14.00	16.31	17.11	18.22				
	10.45	13.00	14.15	14.55	15.36	15.54	18.06	18.58					
✕	10.45	15.00	16.00			17.06	18.26	19.05	19.47	20.43	21.17	21.46	The Talisman
	12.45	14.14	17.10	17.37	18.09	17.51	19.52	20.35	21.30	00.40	01.21	03.05	The North Briton
✕	13.15	15.22	19.20	19.48	20.23	19.11	22.16	23.01					
	16.23	17.48	20.20	20.54	21.33	21.28	00.02	00.58	01.50	02.57	03.39	05.13	The Night Capitals
	16.23	18.20	22.30	22.57	23.39	22.52						05.51	
E	18.10	19.00	22.30	23.19	23.54	01u02	01.53	02.49	03.28	04.19	04.57	06.28	
E	19.20	21.30	23.10			01.06						06.40	The Night Scotsman
E	20.15	21.30	00.01S			02.07		03s33	04s31	04s51	05s29	06.50	
E	21.20	22.00										07.06	The Night Aberdonian
	21u57	22.30											
	22.52												

Notes

Services shown in bold type are through "Inter-City" trains whilst those in light type are connectional timings, indicating that a change of train, en route, will be necessary.

- A Until 25 October
- E Takes Sleeping Car passengers only
- FO Fridays only
- J Until 26 October
- M Until 12 October
- S Sleeping accommodation from Edinburgh is available only for passengers to Peteborough

- h Until 12 October takes passengers for South of Newcastle only
- j Second class only
- s Stops to set down only
- ✕ 1st and 2nd class sleepers
- ⊖ Restaurant service
- ✕ Light refreshments, snacks and hot dishes to order } Available for whole or part of the journey
- □ Cold snacks and drinks

Information subject to alteration without notice

*The number of passengers carried is limited to the seating capacity of the train — all seats reservable.

△ *Note*: This timetable is no longer in operation.

7 You want to arrive in London before six o'clock in the evening. Which would be the best train to take from Aberdeen?
_____.

8 You suddenly decide to go to London tomorrow. Why might it be rather difficult to travel on the 10.00 and the 16.00 trains from Edinburgh?
_____.

9 If you caught the 18.20 from Dundee and travelled through to London, how would you probably feel at 5.13 the next morning, and why?
_____.

10 How many different trains would you travel on between Glasgow and Darlington, leaving Glasgow at 11.00?
___3___.

11 If you were travelling from Edinburgh to London, on which trains would you have to change in order to reach your destination?
_____.

Exercise 102

On the next page are some points for and against living in four different kinds of accommodation. *Using only the information given*, write the discussion between Mr and Mrs Clifford, an elderly couple who are trying to decide whether or not to move from their present house. You should include in the conversation some discussion of each of the four different kinds of accommodation (but not necessarily *all* the points given under each heading).

- **Present house**
  too big – expensive to heat and maintain
  housework too much as getting older
  garden too big
  too far from shops
  sell for good price

- **Mobile home** (a caravan that cannot be moved from its site)
  cheap to buy (so money left to live on or invest)
  easy and cheap to heat, clean and decorate
  no stairs
  well-designed so everything convenient
  no room for own furniture, etc.
  can't have children/grandchildren to stay

- **Flat**
  no garden
  problems with neighbours – noise from TV, etc.
  no outside maintenance problems – painting, repairs, etc.
  feel restricted after freedom of own house
  unless on ground floor, stairs or lifts can be problem

- **Bungalow** (a one-storey house)
  maintenance high – like a house
  good for old people – no stairs
  difficult to find, because everyone wants one
  expensive, because demand exceeds supply
  garden

Write about 200 words, in dialogue form. The beginning of the conversation has been written for you.

MR CLIFFORD: The main problem about staying here is that it's really too much work for us at our age, isn't it?

MRS CLIFFORD: _____.

Exercise 103

On the next page are some entries from the diary of Clare Sneeze. Using the information given, complete the letter that Clare is writing to her mother.

MONDAY 18TH JANUARY

Very quiet day. Work as usual, lunch with Peter. Boring afternoon - Millie away, so helped with letters. Evening - Peter came round. Watched Panorama - v. interesting on nuclear disarmament.
Bath and Bed.
N.B. Must get to sales before end of week.

TUESDAY 19TH JANUARY

Terrible day! Woke late, missed bus, arrived at office 10.30. Boss furious! Promised to stay over lunch hour, so can't meet Peter for lunch. Rang him when things were quiet - boss caught me making personal telephone call - furious again! 12.00 Board meeting - forgot notebook & had to keep them waiting while borrowed Jill's.
Then pencil broke twice.
Home late - raining, so soaked as forgot umbrella in rush this morning. Bed early - headache.

WEDNESDAY 20TH JANUARY

Better! Mr Beesnees decided to visit Manchester branch on spur of moment & asked me to come: Rolls to Gatwick, with me taking notes for Mr. B on way, then company plane.
V. short journey: arr. Manchester 11.15. Managed an hour at shops while Mr B inspected factory & found marvellous pair of shoes for only £10! Back in London 6.15, & Mr B dropped me off at home, which was nice of him! Dinner with Peter (Golden Yashmak).
Bed Midnight.

Dear Mum,

Well, another week has passed, and I promised to keep you up-to-date, so here's my weekly report! Monday was pretty quiet ......

After such a quiet start, Tuesday was a bit of a shock! To start with ......

The board meeting was not much better either! ......

When I got up on Wednesday, I thought things could only get better, and I was right! Mr Beesnees asked me ......

When we arrived in Manchester, ...

When we got back to London, the day ended with ......

That's it for now. See you next weekend.

Love Clare

Appendices

Appendix 1 Word + preposition combinations

Verbs

accuse someone of
agree with
apologise for
apply for
approve of
argue with/about
arrest someone for

believe in
belong to
blame someone for
boast about
borrow something from someone

charge someone with
choose between
comment on
compare with
complain about
concentrate on
congratulate on
consist of

decide on
depend on
disagree with
disapprove of

excuse someone for

face up to
forgive someone for

hear of/about

insist on
interfere with

joke about

Adjectives

according to
accustomed to
afraid of
annoyed with/about/at
anxious about
ashamed of
astonished at
attached to
aware of

capable of
characteristic of
conscious of
crazy about
curious about

delighted at/about
different from
dissatisfied with
doubtful about

enthusiastic about
envious of
excited about

famous for
fed up with
fond of
frightened of
friendly with

good at
guilty of

incapable of
interested in

jealous of

keen on
kind to

Nouns

advantage of
attack on
attitude towards

comparison between
connection between
cruelty towards

decrease in
delay in
difference between/of
difficulty in/with
disadvantage of

expert at/in

(no) hope for

increase in
information about
(have no) intention of

knowledge of

APPENDIX 1

Verbs	Adjectives	Nouns
laugh at		lack of
lend something to someone		
listen to		
long for		
mistake someone for	married to	
		need for
		(take no) notice of
object to	opposed to	opinion of
pay for	pleased with	pleasure in
praise someone for	popular with	preference for
prepare for	proud of	protection from
present someone with	puzzled by/about	
prevent someone from		
protest at/about		
provide someone with		
punish someone for		
quarrel about		
refer to	related to	reaction to
rely on	respected for	reason for
result in	responsible for	reduction in
	rid of	report on
		result of
		rise in
		room for
save someone from	safe from	solution to
sentence someone to	satisfied with	
smile at	sensitive to(wards)	
succeed in	serious about	
suffer from	sick of	
stand for	similar to	
	sorry for/about	
	suspicious of	
	sympathetic to(wards)	
talk to someone about something	tired of	trouble with
thank someone for	typical of	
think of/about		
	unaware of	use of
	used to	
wait for		
warn someone about		
worry about		

Appendix 2 Preposition + word phrases

at breakfast/lunch, etc.
at church/school
at all costs
at ease
at first
at first sight
at a glance
at a guess
at home
at last
at the latest
at least
at a loss
at once
at peace/war
at present
at a profit
at any rate
at random
at sea
at the same time
at times
at work

by accident
by bus/car/plane/etc.
by chance
by day/night
by far
by hand
by heart
by land/sea/air
by all means
by means of
by mistake
by name
by oneself
by post/airmail
by request
by sight
by surprise
by yourself

for ages/ever
for a change
for good
for hire
for life
for love
for nothing
for once
for short
for someone's sake
for a visit/holiday
for a while

from time to time

in addition
in advance
in agreement with
in all
in bed
in any case
in charge
in common
in danger
in the dark
in debt
in the end
in fact
in favour of
in flames
in general
in half/two
in honour of
in a hurry
in ink/pencil
in someone's interest
in length/width etc.
in love
in a ... mood
in mourning
in the news
in pain
in particular
in pieces
in place
in practice/theory
in prison
in private/public
in some respects
in return
in the right/wrong
in safety
in secret
in self-defence
in sight
in stock
in tears
in time
in touch
in town
in tune
in turn
in uniform
in use
in vain
in a way
in other words

in writing

on account of
on behalf of
on business
on a diet
on duty
on fire
on foot
on the one hand
on the other hand
on holiday
on a journey
on the increase
on loan
on one's mind
on order
on purpose
on the radio/TV/tape
on sale
on second thoughts
on strike
on time
on trial
on the whole

out of breath
out of control
out of danger
out of date
out of doors
out of order
out of place
out of practice
out of print
out of the question
out of reach
out of sight
out of stock
out of turn
out of work

off colour
off duty

under age
under one's breath
under control
under discussion
under repair

up to date

without fail
without success
without warning

Appendix 3 Word building

Concrete Noun	Abstract Noun	Verb	Adjective
	(in)ability	enable	(un)able
	absence		absent
	acceptance	accept	(un)acceptable
	accident		accidental
	accommodation	accommodate	
	accuracy		(in)accurate
	accusation	accuse	
	achievement	achieve	
actor/actress	act/action/activity	act	(in)active
	addition	add	additional
administrator	administration	administer	administrative
admirer	admiration	admire	admirable
	admission	admit	
advertiser	advertisement	advertise	
	advice	advise	(in)advisable
	affection	affect	affectionate
	(dis)agreement	(dis)agree	(dis)agreeable
	aim	aim	aimless
	allowance	(dis)allow	
	ambition		(un)ambitious
	amusement	amuse	amusing
	analysis	analyse	
	anger		angry
announcer	announcement	announce	
	annoyance	annoy	annoying/-ed
	anxiety		anxious
	apology	apologise	
	appeal	appeal	appealing
	(dis)appearance	(dis)appear	
applicant	application	apply	
	(dis)appointment	(dis)appoint	(dis)appointing/-ed
	(dis)approval	(dis)approve	
	argument	argue	
	arrangement	arrange	
	arrival	arrive	
artist	art		(in)artistic
assistant	assistance	assist	
	association	associate	
	astonishment	astonish	astonishing/-ed
attendant	attendance	attend	
	attention	attend	(in)attentive
	attraction	attract	(un)attractive
	basis	base	basic
	beauty		beautiful
		bear	(un)bearable
beggar	begging	beg	
	(mis)behaviour	(mis)behave	
	(dis)belief	(dis)believe	
	bitterness		bitter

Concrete Noun	Abstract Noun	Verb	Adjective
blood		bleed	bloody
bomber	bombing	bomb	
	boredom	bore	boring/-ed
boy	boyhood		boyish
	bravery		brave
	breakage	break	broken
breath		breathe	
		brighten	bright
	breadth	broaden	broad
builder/building		build	
calculator		calculate	
	calmness	calm	calm
	cancellation	cancel	
	(in)capacity		(in)capable
	care/carefulness/carelessness	care	careful/careless
	caution		cautious
	celebration	celebrate	
	centre		central
	(un)certainty		(un)certain
	character		(un)characteristic
child/children	childhood		childish
	choice	choose	chosen
circle		circle	circular
	civilisation	civilise	(un)civilised
	classification	classify	classified
cloth/clothes/clothing		clothe	
collector	collection	collect	
	combination	combine	combined
	(dis)comfort	comfort	(un)comfortable
	commerce		commercial
	communication	communicate	(un)communicative
companion	company	accompany	
	comparison	compare	comparative
competitor	competition	compete	competitive
	complaint	complain	
	completion	complete	(in)complete
	complication	complicate	(un)complicated
composer	composition	compose	
	concentration	concentrate	
	conclusion	conclude	
	confidence		confidential/confident
	confusion	confuse	confusing/-ed
	congratulations	congratulate	
	connection	(dis)connect	
conqueror	conquest	conquer	
	conscience/consciousness		(un)conscious
	conservation	conserve	
	consideration	consider	(in)considerate
	construction	construct	(un)constructive
container	contents	contain	
continent			continental
	continuity	continue	continuous

APPENDIX 3

Concrete Noun	Abstract Noun	Verb	Adjective
controller	control	control	(un)controlled
	convenience		(in)convenient
cook/cooker	cooking	cook	
	co-operation	co-operate	(un)co-operative
	correction	correct	(in)correct
correspondent	correspondence	correspond	
	courage/encouragement	(en)(dis) courage	courageous
coward			cowardly
creator	creation	create	creative
criminal	crime		criminal
critic	criticism	criticise	(un)critical
	cruelty		cruel
	cultivation	cultivate	(un)cultivated
	culture		cultural
	curiosity		curious
	danger		dangerous
	darkness	darken	dark
	deafness	deafen	deaf
dealer		deal	
debtor	debt		
	(in)decision	decide	(in)decisive
	declaration	declare	
decorator	decoration	decorate	decorative
	depth	deepen	deep
defender	defence	defend	defensive
	delivery	deliver	
	democracy		(un)democratic
dependant	dependence	depend	(in)dependent/dependable
descendant	descent	descend	
	description	describe	descriptive
	despair	despair	desperate
	destruction	destroy	destructive
	determination	determine	determined
	development	develop	developing
dictator	dictation	dictate	
	difference	differ	different
	difficulty		difficult
director/directory	direction	direct	(in)direct
discoverer	discovery	discover	
	discussion	discuss	discursive
	dismissal	dismiss	
	distance		distant
distributor	distribution	distribute	
	disturbance	disturb	disturbing
	division	divide	dividing/-ed
	doubt	doubt	doubtful
	eagerness		eager
	earnings	earn	
economist	economy	economise	(un)economic(al)
	education	educate	educational
	effect		effective

APPENDICES

Concrete Noun	Abstract Noun	Verb	Adjective
	efficiency		efficient
elector	election	elect	
electrician	electricity		electric/electrical
	embarrassment	embarrass	embarrassed
	emotion		emotional
employer/employee	(un)employment	employ	(un)employed
	energy		energetic
engine/engineer	engineering		
	enjoyment	enjoy	(un)enjoyable
entertainer	entertainment	entertain	entertaining
entrance	entry	enter	
	envy	envy	envious
	equality	equal	equal
		equip	
equipment			
	evidence		evident
examiner	examination	examine	
	excitement	excite	exciting/-ed
	exclusion	exclude	exclusive
exhibition		exhibit	
	existence	exist	
	expansion	expand	
	expense		(in)expensive
	experiment	experiment	experimental
	explanation	explain	
	explosion	explode	explosive
explorer	exploration	explore	
	expression	express	
	extension/extent	extend	
	failure	fail	
family			(un)familiar
	fame		(in)famous
	fascination	fascinate	fascinating/-ed
	fashion		(un)fashionable
	fault		faulty/faultless
	favour		favourite/favourable
	fear	fear	fearful/fearless
food		feed	
	fever		feverish
	firmness		firm
	fitness		(un)fit
	flatness	flatten	flat
	flight	fly	
fool		fool	foolish
	force	force	forceful
foreigner			foreign
	forgetfulness	forget	(un)forgetful
	forgiveness	forgive	(un)forgivable
	fortune		(un)fortunate
	freedom	free	free
	frequency		(in)frequent
	freshness	freshen	fresh
friend	friendship		(un)friendly

Concrete Noun	Abstract Noun	Verb	Adjective
	fright	frighten	frightful
furniture		furnish	(un)furnished
	generosity		generous
	gentleness		gentle
	geography		geographical
	geometry		geometrical
governor	government	govern	
	grammar		(un)grammatical
	greed		greedy
	greeting	greet	
	growth	grow	
	habit		habitual
hand	handful	hand	handy
	(un)happiness		(un)happy
	hardness	harden	hard
	harm	harm	harmful/harmless
	health		(un)healthy
heater	heat/heating	heat	hot
	heaviness		heavy
	height	heighten	high
helper/helping	help	help	(un)helpful/helpless
hero/heroine	heroism		heroic
	hesitation	hesitate	
hijacker	hijack	hijack	
historian	history		historic/-al
	hindrance	hinder	
	home		homeless
	(dis)honesty		(dis)honest
	hope	hope	hopeful/hopeless
horizon			horizontal
	hospitality		(in)hospitable
	humanity		(in)human
	humour		humorous
	hunger		hungry
ice			icy
	identification/identity	identify	
	illness		ill
	image/imagination	imagine	(un)imaginative
imitator	imitation	imitate	
immigrant	immigration	immigrate	
	impatience		impatient
	importance		(un)important
	impossibility		impossible
	impression	impress	(un)impressive
	improvement	improve	
	inclusion	include	inclusive
	independence		independent
	indication	indicate	
	industry	industrialise	industrial
	infection	infect	infectious

Concrete Noun	Abstract Noun	Verb	Adjective
	influence	influence	influential
	information	inform	(un)informative
	injury	injure	injured
	innocence		innocent
	inquiry	inquire	
	installation	instal	
instructor	instruction	instruct	
instrument			instrumental
	insurance	insure	(un)insured
	intelligence		(un)intelligent
	intention	intend	(un)intentional
	interest	interest	interesting/-ed
	interference	interfere	
	interpretation	interpret	
	interruption	interrupt	
	introduction	introduce	
inventor	invention	invent	
investigator	investigation	investigate	
investor	investment	invest	
	invitation	invite	
	jealousy		jealous
judge	judgement	judge	judicial
	knowledge	know	knowledgeable
	laughter	laugh	
lawyer	law		(il)legal
leader	leadership	lead	
	length	lengthen	long
library/librarian			
	life/living	live	lively/alive
light	light	lighten	light
	loneliness		lonely
		loosen	loose
	loss	lose	lost
lover	love	love	lovely
		lower	low
	loyalty		loyal
	luck		(un)lucky
	luxury		luxurious
machine	machinery		
	maintenance	maintain	
	majority		major
manager	management	manage	(un)manageable
man	mankind/manhood		manly
	marriage	marry	married
	measurement	measure	
mechanic	mechanism		mechanical
medicine	medicine		medical
member	membership		
	minority		minor
	misery		miserable

APPENDIX 3

Concrete Noun	Abstract Noun	Verb	Adjective
	mixture	mix	mixed
	month		monthly
	morality		(im)moral
mouth	mouthful		
	movement	move	(im)movable
	multiplication	multiply	
murderer	murder	murder	murdered
musician	music		musical
	mystery	mystify	mysterious
native	nation/nationality	nationalise	national
	nature		(un)natural
	necessity/need	need	(un)necessary
neighbour	neighbourhood		neighbourly/ neighbouring
	notice	notice	noticeable
	(dis)obedience	(dis)obey	(dis)obedient
	obligation	oblige	obligatory
	observation	observe	
	occupation	occupy	
offender	offence	offend	(in)offensive
operator	operation	operate	
opponent	opposition	oppose	opposite
	order	order	(dis)orderly
organiser	organisation	organise	
	origin		original
owner	ownership	own	own
	pain		painful
paint/painter/painting	painting	paint	painted
	patience		patient
	payment	pay	payable
pacifist	peace		peaceful
perfectionist	perfection	perfect	(im)perfect
performer	performance	perform	
permit	permission	permit	
	persuasion	persuade	persuasive
philosopher	philosophy		philosophical
photograph/er	photography	photograph	photographic
piano/pianist			
player		play	playful
	pleasure	please	(un)pleasant
poem/poet	poetry		poetic
poison		poison	poisonous
	politeness		(im)polite
politician	politics		political
	pollution	pollute	(un)polluted
	popularity		(un)popular
	possession	possess	possessive
	possibility		possible
	poverty		poor
	power		powerful
	practice	practise	(im)practical

APPENDICES

Concrete Noun	Abstract Noun	Verb	Adjective
	prayer	pray	
	preference	prefer	preferable
	preparation	prepare	(un)prepared
prescription		prescribe	
	presence		present
	preservation	preserve	
	pretence	pretend	
	prevention	prevent	
	pride		proud
	procedure	proceed	
producer/product	production	produce	(un)productive
	profession		professional
	pronunciation	pronounce	unpronounceable
	proof	prove	
	proposal	propose	
	protection	protect	protective
	provision	provide	
	psychology		psychological
	publication	publish	published
	punishment	punish	
	qualification	qualify	(un)qualified
	quietness	quieten	quiet
	reaction	react	
	realisation	realise	
	reality		(un)real
	reason		(un)reasonable
rebel	rebellion	rebel	rebellious
receipt	reception	receive	
	recognition	recognise	(un)recognisable
	recommendation	recommend	
	reduction	reduce	
referee	reference	refer	
	reflection	reflect	
	refreshment	refresh	refreshing
	refusal	refuse	
	region		regional
	regularity	regulate	(ir)regular
relative/relation	relationship	relate	
	relief	relieve	relieved
	religion		religious
	reminder	remind	
	removal	remove	
	repetition	repeat	repetitive
	replacement	replace	(ir)replaceable
representative		represent	(un)representative
	reservation	reserve	reserved
	resignation	resign	
	resistance	resist	(ir)resistible
	response/responsibility	respond	(ir)responsible
	retirement	retire	retired

APPENDIX 3

Concrete Noun	Abstract Noun	Verb	Adjective
	revision	revise	revised
	revolution	revolt	revolutionary
		ripen	ripe
robber	robbery	rob	
	royalty		royal
	sadness		sad
	safety	save	(un)safe
	satisfaction	satisfy	(dis)satisfied
			(un)satisfactory
scientist	science		(un)scientific
	security		(in)secure
	selection	select	
seller	sale	sell	sold
	sense	sense	sensible/(in)sensitive/senseless
	separation	separate	separate
servant	service	serve	
	shame		ashamed
	shape		shapeless
	sharpness	sharpen	sharp
	shortage	shorten	short
	shyness		shy
	sickness		sick
	signature	sign	
	silence		silent
	simplicity	simplify	simple
singer	song/singing	sing	
	skill		skilful/(un)skilled
		slip	slippery
socialist	society/socialism		social/socialist/sociable
	softness	soften	soft
	solution	solve	
	sorrow		sorry/sorrowful
speaker	speech	speak	spoken
specialist	speciality	specialise	special
squatter		squat	
	starvation	starve	starving
	statement	state	
	stiffness	stiffen	stiff
	stillness		still
	stoppage	stop	
	storage	store	
	straightness	straighten	straight
	strength	strengthen	strong
	stupidity		stupid
	success	succeed	(un)successful
	suggestion	suggest	
sun	sunshine		sunny
survivor	survival	survive	
suspect	suspicion	suspect	suspicious
swelling		swell	swollen
	sympathy	sympathise	(un)sympathetic
	system		systematic

APPENDICES

Concrete Noun	Abstract Noun	Verb	Adjective
talker	talk	talk	talkative
technician	technique/technology		technical
	temptation	tempt	
	tendency	tend	
	tension		tense
terrorist	terror/terrorism	terrify	terrible
	thickness	thicken	thick
thinker	thought	think	thoughtful
	thirst		thirsty
	threat	threaten	threatening
	tightness	tighten	tight
	tiredness	tire	tired
		toughen	tough
tourist	tour/tourism	tour	
trader/tradesman	trade	trade	
	tradition		traditional
translator	translation	translate	
	treatment	treat	
	trouble	trouble	troublesome
	truth		(un)true
	trial	try	
	type		typical
typist	typing	type	
	(mis)understanding	understand	understanding
	union/unity	unite	united
	use/usefulness	use	useful/useless
	vacancy	vacate	vacant
	value	value	valuable/valueless
	variation/variety	vary	various
	violence		violent
visitor	visit	visit	
voter	voting/vote	vote	
	warmth	warm	warm
	warning	warn	warning
	waste	waste	wasteful
	weakness	weaken	weak
	wealth		wealthy
weaver	weaving	weave	woven
	weight	weigh	
	width	widen	wide
	wisdom		wise
wool			woollen
	worth		worthless
	year		yearly
youth	youth		young

Test Papers

Set 1

PAPER 1 Reading Comprehension (1 hour)

Section A

In this section you must choose the word or phrase which best completes each sentence. Give one answer only to each question.

1. I ...... I'll see you next week.
   A wish   B hope   C intend   D want

2. The corridor was so ...... that two people could not pass without knocking into each other.
   A small   B big   C large   D narrow

3. If you are unemployed it's very difficult to ...... ends meet.
   A make   B do   C keep   D stop

4. I was ...... to stay the night, although I knew I shouldn't.
   A suggested   B convinced   C persuaded   D decided

5. It was almost impossible to get a taxi; they were much in ...... during the rush hour.
   A demand   B want   C need   D desire

6. I was surprised when I ...... John in the High Street yesterday.
   A ran up   B came into   C ran into   D went into

7. Which is the best ...... for me to follow if I want to get to the airport by ten o'clock?
   A journey   B travel   C route   D crossing

8. You're not seriously suggesting that I should go there alone! You must be pulling my ......
   A wool   B leg   C arm   D legs

9. The ...... of butter has gone up rapidly.
   A prize   B profit   C worth   D price

10. If at first you don't succeed, ... again.
    A attempt   B make   C try   D do

11. We need an umbrella on the beach to give us some ...... at midday.
    A shadow   B shade   C cloud   D dark

12. He chose the ...... for a suit and had it made up by his tailor.
    A cloth   B clothes   C clothing   D textile

13. She lay ...... for hours thinking of the interview she had had that day.
    A wake   B woke   C awake   D awoken

14. When the gunman entered the grocer's shop, the assistant had no ...... but to give him the money.
    A possibility   B excuse   C occasion   D alternative

15. Have you ...... that new shop that has just opened down Campbell Road?
    A remarked   B noticed   C attended   D realised

16. Your seat is number 23. That's in the front ...... on the left.
    A row   B line   C rank   D seat

17. X equals 24 and Y equals 26, ... X + Y equals 50.
    A however   B then   C therefore   D but

18. Immediate steps should be ...... to improve the state of Britain's railways.
    A made   B done   C organised   D taken

19 It was the first time they had ...... in twenty years of marriage but they were the best of friends the following day.
    A fallen down   B fallen out   C broken down   D broken out

20 If you want to make a decision, I think you should listen to both ...... of the argument.
    A edges   B sides   C limits   D borders

21 The Duchess's huge jewellery collection is heavily insured because it is ......
    A worth   B invaluable   C worthless   D priceless

22 The two vases are ...... in shape and design.
    A equal   B same   C similar   D like

23 When she arrived at the meeting-place there was no one there, ... she went back home.
    A then   B so   C as   D when

24 I'm ...... him to arrive at any moment.
    A expecting   B attending   C waiting   D awaiting

25 The new police station is to be built in the ...... of the town hall.
    A near   B neighbourhood   C close   D side

Section B

In this section of Reading Comprehension you will find after each of the passages a number of questions or unfinished statements about the passage, each with four suggested answers or ways of finishing. You must choose the one which you think fits best. **Give one answer only** to each question. Read each passage right through before choosing your answers.

First passage

Mor still stood looking up, as if with the very force of his will he could keep his son from falling. The fire-brigade should be arriving now very soon. Only let their ladder be long enough! Suppose it were not? Or suppose — so intently was his gaze now fixed upon the motionless extended form of Donald, that it was not until he heard a gasp of horror from the crowd who had now stopped their racing to and fro, and were staring upward, that he   (5) transferred his attention to Carde. Carde was swaying. His head had dropped forward and his arm was very very slowly sliding off the parapet. As this arm supported gradually less and less of his weight, he gripped more and more frantically on to the lightning conductor, trying to pass the hand by which he held it through between the conductor and the stone. He had been spreadeagled against the wall. Now he began to swing slowly round,   (10) as one arm moved from the parapet and the other attempted to twine itself about the wire of the conductor. His feet, which had been perched sideways upon the tiny ledge, turned until he was gripping the ledge with his toes. Then Mor saw something terrible. The lightning conductor, now beginning to take most of Carde's weight, was slowly parting company with the wall. But this was not what was, for Mor, the most dreadful. He saw that   (15) the conductor passed upward, over the parapet, across the wider ledge and under his son's body. If the wire were ripped right away it would dislodge Donald from the ledge.

  Mor had not time even to draw a breath at this discovery before Carde fell. The lightning conductor, with a tearing sound which was audible in the tense silence, came away from the wall, and with a sudden heart-rending cry Carde fell backwards, turning over in the   (20) air, and landed with a terrible sound somewhere upon the heap of blankets. A number of boys had run forward in an attempt to break his fall. Confused cries arose, and a strange wailing sound as of a number of people crying. The ambulance was backing across the play-ground. People who were presumably doctors and nurses were clearing a way, helped by Mr Everard and Prewett.   (25)

From *The Sandcastle* by Iris Murdoch

26 What was Mor looking up at?
    A   A long ladder
    B   A crowd of people
    C   The fire brigade
    D   Two people in danger

27 Mor looked away from his son and towards Carde because
    A   he saw Carde move
    B   he heard a gasp of horror
    C   everybody was racing to and fro
    D   he saw Donald move

28 How was Carde managing to support himself?
    A   By swaying to and fro
    B   With one arm
    C   Only by gripping the lightning conductor
    D   With one arm, one hand and his feet

29 The most dreadful thing for Mor was
    A   the thought that Carde might slip and fall
    B   the fact that he could see his son's body
    C   the possibility that Carde's fall might bring Mor's son down too
    D   the fact that the conductor passed upward

30 When Carde fell
    A   there was complete silence
    B   he gave a tearing sound
    C   he cried out as he fell
    D   Mor drew in his breath

31 Immediately after Carde's fall
    A   quite a lot of noise could be heard
    B   a lot of blankets were placed where he fell
    C   nurses and doctors crowded round him
    D   the wailing sound of an ambulance was heard

Second passage

I had been walking for a few minutes when I was stopped dead by the appearance of a set of deep tracks coming down the mountainside on the left of the valley. I realized immediately that this was the exact point where this whatever-it-was had dropped down behind the ridge the previous evening. The snow had been very soft and whatever it was had made deep tracks in a similar manner to ourselves. Anyhow, I took a picture of the (5) tracks going up the mountainside and called Mike over. There were one or two scratch-marks like claw-marks on the snow, and Mike said, 'Oh, it's a bear.'
   But there were one or two things that didn't look like a bear to me. I didn't form any opinions at that stage but just looked at all the tracks and the features. It wasn't possible to get a picture of one clear footprint because the snow had tumbled into each hole, which (10) was at least 30 cm. deep. I thought they were about the size of a small man, about my own size foot, which is size six. We then carried on a little farther up the valley but by this time the cloud had come down and we couldn't really see the South Face of Annapurna, so Mike and I went back to the camp and rejoined the Sherpas. I examined the tracks

through the binoculars and estimated that they came down to an altitude of around (15)
4,500 metres, and vanished over the crest of the ridge at about 5,000 metres.

That night, after Mike had departed, I began to ponder about the tracks. It did occur to me that it was possible that this creature, whatever it was, might still be around, so I stuck my head outside the tent. It was bright moonlight and the moon was shining straight on to the hillside where the tracks were. It was even possible to read small print, it was so (20) bright. The hillside had gentle undulations, rather like an easy ski slope, and I made a mental note of where I could see dark spots which were possibly rocks or trees. If any of these moved they could only be some kind of living creatures. It was a fantastically cold night – I was in two sleeping bags but was still cold. Even so I kept my head sticking outside the tent, and after a time noticed that one of these dark spots appeared to have (25) moved. I couldn't be sure, but I continued watching and then, without a doubt, it started to move quite quickly. There was a monocular in the tent which I focused on the dark, moving shape. It was then that I could definitely distinguish limbs and a kind of bounding movement. It was going directly uphill towards another clump of trees, and it was obvious, just by the movements, that it was a reasonably powerful animal and that it was bounding (30) along on all fours.

From *Annapurna South Face* by Chris Bonington, extract by Don Whillans

32 Why was the writer especially interested in the tracks?
    A Because they were very deep
    B Because he had no idea how they might have been made
    C Because of the scratch marks
    D Because he thought he might already have seen the creature that had made them

33 The footprints were
    A similar to those of a man
    B similar in size to those of a man
    C similar to those made by the writer's feet
    D very clear

34 Why did they go back to the camp?
    A Because they wanted to look at the tracks
    B Because of the altitude
    C To rejoin the Sherpas
    D Because of the weather

35 That night
    A the author spent his time reading
    B the author looked out of the tent in order to see the moon
    C the moon made it possible to see clearly
    D the author kept putting his head in and out of the tent

36 He carefully noted all the dark spots
    A in case one of them might be the creature
    B because they were rocks or trees
    C because one of them had moved
    D in case he wanted to go skiing later

Third passage

HOW SAFE ARE YOUR VALUABLES?

Think about all the things in your home which are of special importance to you and your family. They may be items of particular sentimental value which would be virtually impossible to replace. Or other property which could be replaced if necessary – but at a price.

To a thief or burglar they're just another way of making easy cash.

Naturally, safeguarding your home against the thief is the best protection of all. But if someone *did* break in and steal something, could you describe your property to the police – fully and accurately?

Every year hundreds of thousands of pounds worth of lost or stolen property is recovered by the police and not returned to its rightful owners, simply because it can't be properly identified.

MAKE SURE YOUR PROPERTY REALLY IS UNIQUE

You can do this by marking each item in a special way and in a special place. That way if your property is ever lost or stolen you stand a much better chance of getting it back again.

Use your postcode followed by your house number or the first two letters of its name to identify each article. Eg. a person living at 13 Chester Street, Anytown, AN1 2ZG would use AN1 2ZG 13. If you don't know your postcode, ask at your local post office.

Property can be marked by etching, die-stamping, branding, identification paint or by security marker pen which uses invisible ink and can only be read under an ultra-violet lamp. In case of difficulty your local crime prevention officer can advise you.

Remember, all marking should be done wherever possible on a hidden surface, otherwise it may be removed or defaced by a thief.

MAKE DOUBLY SURE – KEEP A RECORD OF YOUR PROPERTY

Of course there may be some items of property which you cannot mark. But you can still help the police – and yourself – by keeping a record of them.

A simple and effective way of doing this is to photograph each object, paying particular attention to distinguishing marks such as initials, crests, hallmarks or any other form of identity. It is useful to lay a ruler alongside the article being photographed to give an accurate scale of the object.

Finally, use the space on this leaflet to keep a record of the items you have post-coded and where the marks are. It's a good idea to leave a second copy of the list and photo negatives on different premises with a responsible person.

If you would like advice on any aspect of marking or protecting your property, contact your local crime prevention officer. His advice will cost you nothing. But one day it could save you a great deal.

37 The general aim of this leaflet is to help people to
   A   discourage thieves or burglars from stealing property
   B   make their property easy to recognise if it is found after being stolen
   C   help the police to catch people who steal property
   D   stop their property from being stolen

38 The action should be taken
   A   after the property has been recovered
   B   as soon as the property is lost or stolen
   C   immediately the police notify the rightful owners
   D   before the property is stolen

39 You should protect *all* the things which are important to you
   A   by contacting your local crime prevention officer
   B   by marking them on a hidden surface
   C   by making sure you can identify them clearly
   D   by taking photographs of them

40 Getting further advice about how to mark and safeguard your property should cost you
   A   a great deal of money
   B   a small amount of money
   C   nothing at all
   D   hundreds of thousands of pounds.

PAPER 2 Composition (1½ hours)

Write **two only** of the following composition exercises. Your answers must follow exactly the instructions given, and must be of between 120 and 180 words each.

1. Write a letter to a friend explaining why you have not written for a long time, and inviting him/her to a party in your house. Give him/her instructions as to how to get to your house. You should make the beginning and ending like those of an ordinary letter, but the address is not to be counted in the number of words.

2. Tell the story of your favourite book **or** film and say why you like it.

3. You found a very old suitcase and you spent an afternoon looking through it. Describe clearly **three** of the articles you found in the case.

4. 'Smoking should be banned in all public places.' Do you agree with this? If so, say why; if not, say why not.

5. Base your answer to the following question on your reading of *any* book which you have read recently, or know well.*

   Referring closely to incidents in the book, describe the part played in the story by two characters other than the most important ones.

PAPER 3 Use of English (2 hours)

1. Fill each of the numbered blanks in the following passage. Use only **one** word in each space.

Paul Sherlock (1) .... the house and strode across the fields. (2) .... it was snowing (3) ...., he wanted to get out into the fresh air. (4) .... the last week he had spent (5) .... too long inside, trying to find the answer (6) .... the question — who had murdered Sir Stan. (7) .... of the servants appeared to have any reason for killing him, nor (8) .... his children. He thought that the murderer (9) .... have been Lady Hilda, (10) .... story of where she had been on the night of the murder he did not believe. But, (11) .... to everyone he had talked (12) ...., they were a devoted couple. Paul's other problem was to find out exactly how Sir Stan had (13) .... killed. The doctor said that he had been stabbed, but certainly not with a knife or any metal (14) .... (15) .... far, Paul Sherlock had (16) .... little progress on this case, and he was (17) .... that the fresh air (18) .... clear his brain and let him think better.

He stopped to look (19) .... the frozen lake and (20) .... he knew the answer — it was an icicle that the murderer had used to kill Sir Stan!!

2. Finish each of the following sentences in such a way that it means exactly the same as the sentence before it.

   Example:
   I haven't enjoyed myself so much for years.

   Answer: It's years since I enjoyed myself so much.

   a) 'Don't you think you should go to bed earlier? You look so tired,' she said to Alison.
      She suggested ....

   b) I haven't spoken French for ages.
      It's ages ....

   c) The cinema was such a long way from the city centre that no-one went there.
      The cinema was so ....

*The prescribed books on which this type of question is based will vary from year to year.

d) 'You'll have to leave this school unless you arrive on time,' the principal told him.
He was... *warned by the principle to leave that school unless he arrived on time*
(handwritten above: *He was warned to arrive on time, otherwise he would leave*)

e) There's a white table in the middle of the room.
The table ...*in the middle of the room is white*

f) 'Is it all right if I smoke?'
Would you mind ...*if ?I smoked*

g) She hardly ever goes swimming nowadays.
She doesn't ...*often go swimming nowadays*

h) Keep quiet, or I'll scream.
Unless ...*you keep quite, I'll scream*

i) You really have got beautiful hair.
What ...*beautiful hair you've got*

j) It's more expensive than it was.
It's not ...*cheaper*
so (as) cheap as

3 The word in capitals at the end of each of the following sentences can be used to form a word that fits suitably in the blank space. Fill each blank in this way.

Example:
He said 'Good morning' in a most friendly way.   FRIEND

a) The ...... between the workers and the management broke down.   AGREE

b) How can you sit in that position for so long? It looks terribly ....   COMFORT

c) The pianist gave a ...... performance, playing everything perfectly.   FAULT

d) Let's use this room for studying. It's ...... quiet.   COMPARE

e) If at first you don't ......, try again.   SUCCESS

f) He has decided to be a ...... when he grows up.   POLITICS

g) The pain from his broken leg was almost ......, and the doctor had to give him a pain-killing injection.   BEAR

h) Everybody agrees that he is a very charming and ...... person.   LIKE

i) The engineers' report emphasised that they would have to ...... the bridge before it could be reopened.   STRONG

j) Although I do not share his religious ......, I respect them.   BELIEVE

4 Make all the changes and additions necessary to produce, from the following seven sets of words and phrases, seven sentences which together make a complete letter from Hiroko to Mrs Mitchell. Note carefully from the example what kinds of alteration need to be made.

Example:
I/wonder/why you/not/reply/last letter
Answer: I was wondering why you had not replied to my last letter.

Dear Mrs Mitchell,
a) It be/lovely hear/from you again/after/long time. *(such a)*
b) It/seem ages/I/be/England/with you.
c) I often think/good time/we have/and wonder/the children/get on/school.
d) My brother/think/come/England/study/next year.

e) I/give him/your address/and I know/he/try/call/see/you.
f) Oh, I forget/mention/I get married/next year/Toshi/ – remember/one/come/visit me/frequently.
g) Please write again soon/I love/hear/news.
   With love,
    Hiroko

5. Below is the programme for a weekend excursion organised by your school, together with some notes about the places which were visited. You and several fellow-students went on the trip, and enjoyed it very much. The week **after** the excursion, a friend who did not accompany you asked you various questions about your trip. **Using only the information given below**, write the answers you gave to his questions. You will probably need 50–60 words for each answer.

Saturday
09.00 Leave Camford by coach
10.30 Coffee in Burtree-on-Whenn
11.30 Leave Burtree: drive through Cotvern Hills
13.00 Arrive Brisport. Check in at King Edward Hotel. Lunch
    Afternoon free for shopping and sightseeing in Brisport
19.00 Leave King Edward Hotel for Southville Stadium: dog-racing, dinner, disco and cabaret
01.00 (approx) return to hotel

Sunday
08.30–09.30 Breakfast
10.00 Coach leaves Brisport
11.00 Chilton Gorge and Caves
12.30 Lunch at 'Hunk of Cheese'
13.30 Coach leaves Chilton
16.00 Tea in Salcaster. Time to visit Cathedral
18.30 (approx) Arrive Camford

Notes

Burtree-on-Whenn
Picturesque village in Cotvern Hills: River Whenn runs alongside main street crossed by little stone bridges. Many craft shops, gift shops, etc. Small local history museum.

Brisport
Busy commercial city on River Nyne, its hilly setting nevertheless makes it one of the most beautiful towns in England. A popular place from which to explore the nearby Cotvern and Mendock Hills. Excellent shopping and entertainments centre.

King Edward Hotel, Brisport
Delightfully situated on cliff overlooking River Nyne, yet convenient for town centre, shops and entertainments. A modernised sixteenth-century hotel combining old world charm with comfort and good service. 40 rooms, 10 with private bath; French and English cooking. Parties catered for. Car park at back.

Southville Stadium
Brisport's sporting and entertainment centre: football, motor-cycle speedway, dog-racing. Visit the famous Garter Room panoramic restaurant and enjoy a spectacular view of the

> evening's racing over a first-class four-course dinner. Visit the 'Dog's Life' disco and cabaret for dancing and entertainment by our resident group 'The Flying Osbornes'.
>
> *Chilton*
> Pretty village deep in famous Chilton Gorge, impressive narrow valley whose cliff walls rise up to 200 metres high around village. Rock-climbing, caves, antique shops, fifteenth-century church and motor museum.
>
> *Salcaster*
> Roman town with fine thirteenth-century cathedral – 140-metre spire is highest in country – and many other fine old buildings.

a) I've never been to Brisport. What's it like? Is there anything to do or see around there?

b) Tell me how you spent your time on Saturday evening and where you stayed.

c) Did you notice any differences between Burtree-on-Whenn and Chilton?

d) I don't suppose *every* moment of your time was organised for you. What opportunities did you have to go off and do things by yourself?

Set 2

PAPER 1 Reading Comprehension (1 hour)

Section A

In this section you must choose the word of phrase which best completes each sentence. Give one answer only to each question.

1. Two hundred pounds is too much for that coat. It's just not ...... it.
   A value   B worth   C deal   D bargain

2. ...... it was extremely cold, the explorers decided to sleep without tents.
   A As   B Despite   C Although   D Because

3. Come on, hurry up! Stop ...... time.
   A wasting   B spending   C losing   D passing

4. The car swerved to avoid the cyclist, but unfortunately he was ...... his bike.
   A run over   B knocked down   C knocked off   D run into

5. It took years of research, but ...... they found the answer.
   A at the end   B lastly   C presently   D in the end

6. The factory ...... called his managers together for a meeting.
   A principal   B boss   C chef   D leader

7. She lived in the little ivy-covered cottage ...... the tall trees of the forest.
   A among   B between   C in   D before

8. He was on the ...... of collapse when the search party found him.
   A edge   B limit   C near   D point

9. The result left him in ...... that Chalmers would make an excellent leader.
   A no need   B no fear   C no doubt   D no chance

10. The play was so sad that the audience ...... into tears.
    A burst   B broke   C went   D fell

11. I'm looking for a school with a ...... attitude towards its students and their work.
    A heavy   B hard   C serious   D grave

12. The winter snow took longer than usual to ....
    A dissolve   B go off   C fall down   D melt

13. He took swimming lessons, but ...... he never learnt to enjoy the water.
    A therefore   B unfortunately   C happily   D although

14. You have a marvellous ...... of the whole island from the top of the tower.
    A scene   B scenery   C vision   D view

15. The paper ...... has been caused by a strike of the distributors.
    A decrease   B lack   C loss   D shortage

16. Where are you calling from? I can hardly hear you. Your voice is terribly ....
    A faint   B pale   C faded   D dull

17. I wish my father would ...... down and get a good, steady job.
    A settle   B order   C retire   D set

18. Don't ...... the jug right up, otherwise it'll spill when you pick it up.
    A fell   B full   C fill   D feel

19 The lecture will begin at 9.00 ....
    A punctual   B on time   C in time   D sharp

20 His mother told him not to let ...... of her hand when they got into the crowd.
    A loose   B go   C out   D hold

21 The snow was falling so fast that the train had ...... in getting to its destination.
    A problem   B troubles   C difficulty   D annoyance

22 Would you ...... the table for me, please?
    A lay   B lie   C lain   D laid

23 Under no ...... should you press that red button, Stevie ... Stevie!!
    A account   B consideration   C occasion   D circumstances

24 The group ...... of thirteen people.
    A contains   B composes   C consists   D comprises

25 People can sometimes feel very ...... in a crowded city.
    A lone   B only   C lonely   D sole

Section B

In this section of Reading Comprehension you will find after each of the passages a number of questions or unfinished statements about the passage, each with four suggested answers or ways of finishing. You must choose the one which you think fits best. Give **one answer only** to each question. Read each passage right through before choosing your answers.

First passage

He put on his goggles, fitted them tight, tested the vacuum. His hands were shaking. Then he chose the biggest stone he could carry and slipped over the edge of the rock until half of him was in the cool, enclosing water and half in the hot sun. He looked up once at the empty sky, filled his lungs once, twice, and then sank fast to the bottom with the stone. He let it go and began to count. He took the edges of the hole in his hands and drew himself   (5)
into it, wriggling his shoulders in sideways as he remembered he must, kicking himself along with his feet.

Soon he was clear inside. He was in a small rock-bound hole filled with yellowish-grey water. The water was pushing him up against the roof. The roof was sharp and pained his back. He pulled himself along with his hands — fast, fast — and used his legs as levers. His   (10)
head knocked against something; a sharp pain dizzied him. Fifty, fifty-one, fifty-two ...... He was without light, and the water seemed to press upon him with the weight of rock. Seventy-one, seventy-two ...... There was no strain on his lungs. He felt like an inflated balloon, his lungs were so light and easy, but his head was pulsing.

He was being continually pressed against the sharp roof, which felt slimy as well as   (15)
sharp. Again he thought of octopuses, and wondered if the tunnel might be filled with weed that could tangle him. He gave himself a panicky, convulsive kick forward, ducked his head, and swam. His feet and hands moved freely, as if in open water. The hole must have widened out. He thought he must be swimming fast, and he was frightened of banging his head if the tunnel narrowed.   (20)

A hundred, a hundred and one ...... The water paled. Victory filled him. His lungs were beginning to hurt. A few more strokes and he would be out. He was counting wildly; he said a hundred and fifteen, and then, a long time later, a hundred and fifteen again. The water was a clear jewel-green all around him. Then he saw, above his head, a crack running up through the rock. Sunlight was falling through it, showing the clean dark rock   (25)
of the tunnel, a single mussel shell, and darkness ahead.

He was at the end of what he could do. He looked up at the crack as if it were filled with air and not water, as if he could put his mouth to it to draw in air. A hundred and fifteen, he heard himself say inside his head — but he had said that long ago. He must go on into the blackness ahead, or he would drown. His head was swelling, his lungs cracking. A hundred and fifteen, a hundred and fifteen pounded through his head, and he feebly clutched at rocks in the dark, pulling himself forward, leaving the brief space of sunlit water behind. He felt he was dying. He was no longer quite conscious. He struggled on in the darkness between lapses into unconsciousness. An immense, swelling pain filled his head, and then the darkness cracked with an explosion of green light. His hands, groping forward, met nothing, and his feet, kicking back, propelled him out into the open sea. He drifted to the surface, his face turned up to the air. He was gasping like a fish. (30)

(35)

From *Through the Tunnel* by Doris Lessing

26 The boy was pressed against the roof of the tunnel
    A by the weed which entangled him
    B by octopuses
    C by the sharpness of the rocky roof
    D by the force of the water

27 The crack running up through the rock
    A was not wide enough for the boy to swim up
    B meant that the boy was safe at last
    C was completely dark
    D was filled with air and sunlight

28 The boy repeated the number a hundred and fifteen
    A long ago
    B because he was at the end of his swim
    C because he could no longer think clearly
    D because that was the number of rocks he had clutched at

29 It was dark
    A throughout the length of the tunnel
    B under the water
    C only in the last part of the tunnel
    D in parts of the tunnel

30 The boy's head
    A swelled like an inflated balloon
    B was full of air
    C was continually knocking against things
    D had a terrible pain in it

Second passage

In 1849 a servant girl wrote home to her brother from Port Adelaide, South Australia: 'I have accepted a situation at £20 per annum so you can tell the servants in your neighbourhood not to stay in England for such wages as from £4 to £8 a year, but come here.' Letters such as these, which were circulated from kitchen to kitchen and from attic to attic in English homes, were the best recruiting agents for the colonies which were then so (5) desperately in need of young women to serve the pioneers who were trying to create a new life for themselves in their chosen countries. Other girls read about the much better prospects overseas in newspapers and magazines, which also published advertisements, giving details of free or assisted passages, while some servants, like the writer of the letter quoted above, were induced to set forth after attending a public meeting on emigration. (10)

Now that Australia is not much more than a quick phone call and a day's flight away, it is difficult to visualise all the discomforts, deprivations and dangers which young servant girls, and other emigrants, had to face on the long sea voyage a century or so ago. The journey took three to four months, at least, according to the state of the sea and the winds, as clippers continued to be used for reasons of economy well into the age of steam, taking (15) out what seamen called a cargo of 'live lumber' and bringing back another of Australian wool. The emigrants lived together in cramped and often ill-ventilated quarters below deck, sleeping in wooden bunks and eating from tin plates. Whenever there was a particularly violent storm, they were often battened down below, with all their fears, their sickness and the smells, until danger had passed. Some of the women were usually (20) pregnant, so that the passenger lists were often swollen by the time the ships reached port, though these increases were frequently balanced by an equivalent number of deaths among the adult emigrants and their young children.

From *Life Below Stairs* by Frank Huggett

31 What was *most* likely to persuade servants to work in Australia?
   A Public meetings on emigration
   B Advertisements in newspapers and magazines
   C Recruiting agents
   D Personal recommendations from people who had actually gone there

32 Letters such as the one quoted
   A were passed around among servants in England
   B were published in newspapers and magazines
   C were written immediately after public meetings
   D were sent to the colonies

33 The journey to Australia was
   A made by steamship because this was cheaper
   B made by steamship because this was quicker
   C made by sailing ship although this was slower
   D made by sailing ship although this was cheaper

34 The emigrants were treated rather like
   A servants
   B cargo
   C wool
   D Australians

35 During the voyages,
   A passengers often became swollen
   B births and deaths often occurred in similar numbers
   C most of the adults often died
   D the number of passengers increased because of children being born during the voyage

Third passage

United Kingdom Customs

The Customs officer is legally entitled to examine your luggage. Please co-operate with him if he asks to examine it. You are responsible for opening, unpacking and repacking your luggage.

Notes on allowances

1. The countries of the EEC (Common Market) are Belgium, Denmark, France, West Germany, Greece, Irish Republic, Italy, Luxembourg, the Netherlands, Portugal, Spain and the United Kingdom (but not the Channel Islands).

2. Whisky, gin, rum, brandy, vodka and most liqueurs normally exceed 22% vol. (38.8° proof) but advocaat, cassis, fraise, suze and aperitifs may be less.

If you have nothing more than the allowances and no prohibited or restricted goods or goods for commercial purposes, go straight through the channel indicated by the green symbol — unless you are asked to stop by an officer.

If you have more than the allowances listed or if you have prohibited or restricted goods or goods for commercial purposes, you must declare them to an officer. Go into the channel indicated by the red symbol.

Duty and tax free allowances

You are entitled to the allowances in either of the columns below (but not both) for any category of goods, as represented by the boxes.

COLUMN 1	COLUMN 2
Goods obtained duty and tax free in the EEC, or duty and tax free on a ship or aircraft, or goods obtained outside the EEC.	Goods obtained duty and tax paid in the EEC.
Tobacco products 200 cigarettes or 100 cigarillos — double if you live outside Europe or 50 cigars or 250 grammes of tobacco	**Tobacco products** 300 cigarettes or 150 cigarillos or 75 cigars or 400 grammes of tobacco
Alcoholic drinks 1 litre of alcoholic drinks over 22% vol. (38.8° proof) or 2 litres of alcoholic drinks not over 22% vol. or fortified or sparkling wine plus 2 litres of still table wine	**Alcoholic drinks** 1½ litres of alcoholic drinks over 22% vol. (38.8° proof) or 3 litres of alcoholic drinks not over 22% vol. or fortified or sparkling wine plus 5 litres of still table wine

Persons under 17 are not entitled to tobacco and drinks allowances

Perfume 50 grammes (60 cc or 2 fl oz)	**Perfume** 75 grammes (90 cc or 3 fl oz)
Toilet water 250 cc (9 fl oz)	**Toilet water** 375 cc (13 fl oz)
Other goods £32 worth	**Other goods** £250 worth

If you are visiting the United Kingdom for less than six months, you are also entitled to bring in, free of duty and tax, all personal effects (except tobacco products, alcoholic drinks, perfume and toilet water) which you intend to take with you when you leave.

36 You should not go through the green channel
   A if you have 200 cigarettes and one litre of alcohol
   B if you have made no purchases abroad
   C if you are 16 years old and have 50 cc of perfume
   D if you are 16 years old and have 200 cigarettes

37 If you go through the green channel
   A you may be stopped by a customs officer
   B you will be stopped by a customs officer
   C you will not be stopped by a customs officer
   D you should stop and ask a customs officer if you may go straight through

38 You must go through the red channel
   A if you are visiting the UK from abroad
   B if you are a businessman carrying goods which you intend to sell in the UK
   C if you are over 17 and have more than 1 litre of still table wine
   D if you have obtained any goods outside the EEC   *European Economic Community*

39 Returning to the UK from a holiday in the Channel Islands, you are allowed duty-free
   A up to 350 cigarettes
   B up to 300 cigarettes
   C up to 200 cigarettes
   D as many cigarettes as you like

40 Which of the following should go through the green channel?
   A A 10-year-old American boy travelling direct from France, bringing in a 60 cc bottle of perfume and 300 cigarettes
   B A 20-year-old Indonesian student travelling direct from Bahrain, bringing in 100 cigarellos and 1 litre of whisky
   C A 40-year-old Danish businessman travelling direct from South Africa, bringing in 50 cigars and 5 litres of wine
   D An 80-year-old Chinese lady travelling direct from the USA, bringing in 600 cigarettes, 75 cigars, 3 litres of whisky and 6 bottles of perfume

PAPER 2 Composition (1½ hours)

Write **two only** of the following composition exercises. Your answers must follow exactly the instructions given, and must be of between 120 and 180 words each.

1. You are coming to England to study English, and your language school has just sent you the address of the Perrin family, with whom you will be staying. Write a letter to Mrs Perrin introducing yourself and telling her of your travel arrangements. You should make the beginning and ending like those of an ordinary letter, but the address is not to be counted in the number of words.
2. Last week you were going abroad on holiday, but when you arrived at the airport you discovered that no planes were leaving because of bad weather. Describe the scene at the airport.
3. There is a meeting in your town about a proposal to build a multi-storey car park in your street. Some people in the town are in favour and some against. You speak at the meeting on behalf of the residents in the street, all of whom are against the car park. Write the speech you gave.
4. Describe a wedding in your country.
5. Base your answer to the following question on *any* book which you have read recently, or know well.*

   Describe two important happenings in the book, and their significance in the story as a whole.

PAPER 3 Use of English (2 hours)

1. Fill in each of the numbered blanks in the passage with **one** suitable word.

(1) ...... Mrs Grimble turned into Acacia Avenue late one night she saw a crowd of people gathered outside her house. (2) ...... first thought was that she had forgotten to switch (3) ...... the gas and the house had (4) ...... fire, but she quickly realised (5) ...... this was (6) ...... the case as there was no smoke. She hurried anxiously down the avenue, thinking of all the horrible (7) ...... She heard the crowd gasp and some people held up (8) ...... arms, as if to catch something. As she got (9) ...... she saw that (10) ...... was looking up at the tree in the front garden and (11) ......, sitting on one of the thinnest branches, was Tiger, her cat.

   'Thank goodness it's only the cat and not something much (12) ......,' she thought.

   'Mrs Grimble,' said her next-door neighbour, 'your cat (13) ...... woken up the whole street. It has been up that tree (14) ...... two hours, making a terrible noise and nobody can (15) ...... it to come down.'

   Mrs Grimble apologised and disappeared inside the house. A (16) ...... seconds later the crowd was surprised to hear the sound of someone (17) ...... the piano. (18) ...... hesitation the cat came down (19) ...... the tree and walked calmly into the house, leaving the neighbours standing outside looking (20) ...... each other in amazement.

2. Finish each of the following sentences in such a way that it means exactly the same as the sentence printed before it.

   Example:
   It took me an hour to get here today.
   I spent ......

   Answer: I spent an hour getting here today.

*The prescribed books on which this type of question is based will vary from year to year.

a) The men are rebuilding the bridge which collapsed last year.
   The bridge which collapsed last year is being collapsed

b) Your hair really needs cutting.
   You really ought to have your hair cut

c) Mr Pinchley makes his teenage children stay at home in the evenings
   Mr Pinchley won't let his teenage children go out.

d) I regret speaking to him so severely yesterday.
   I wish I hadn't spoken to him so severely yesterday.

e) Take the spare key with you: I think it's possible that you'll be home before me.
   Take the spare key with you in case you are at home before me.

f) 'How many Japanese students are there in your school?' she asked me.
   She asked me how many student were there in my school.

g) I live in a town not far from the capital.
   The town I live in is not far from the capital

h) We don't need to do homework every night.
   It's not necessary for us to do homework every night

i) The spectators cheered loudly every time Jason Foley got the ball.
   The spectators gave ......

j) I've never seen such a bad film as that one.
   That's the worst film I've ever seen.

3 The word in capitals at the end of each of the following sentences can be used to form a word that fits suitably in the blank space. Fill each blank in this way.

Example:
He said 'Good morning' in a most friendly way.   FRIEND

a) The new motorway ...... will be built before 1994.   EXTEND

b) A number of new books has recently ...... from the library.   APPEAR

c) The ...... from the fire could be felt throughout the house.   WARM

d) The room was very ...... decorated, and was admired by everybody.   ATTRACT

e) You can always rely on the train service; it is very ....   DEPEND

f) It was a very ...... situation for everybody.   EMBARRASS

g) Last night's film was one of the most ...... I've ever seen. It was a very good night's entertainment.   ENJOY

h) In ...... with many other countries, England is small.   COMPARE

i) Their ...... on the mountain was attributed to the warm clothes and the tent which they had with them.   SURVIVE

j) The woman strongly ...... of her son's behaviour, and punished him for it.   APPROVE

4 Write out the following passage in dialogue form, making all necessary changes. Begin as shown:

Jackie had the idea of going to the local football match. She said that although the team had not been playing well, she thought this game might be better. She added that in her opinion more people ought to support the local team. Steve asked her if she had ever been to a football match and whether she knew anything about the rules. Jackie was rather surprised at the question and pointed out that she had three brothers!

At this point, Lesley interrupted and said the most important thing for her was how much it would cost, as she had not got a lot of money left. Jackie reassured her that it was quite cheap — certainly less than £5, and so Lesley and Steve both agreed that they should all spend the afternoon together at the local football match. Jackie reminded everyone to wear warm clothes and they arranged to meet outside the stadium at 2.30 that afternoon.

JACKIE: How about going to the local football match?
......
......

5 In the following conversation, Mr Fisher is being interviewed by the Director for a job as the new head of the personnel department. You are at this interview and have been asked by your boss, the present head of the personnel department, to listen to what was said on the following *only*:

a) How Mr Fisher became involved in personnel work.

b) The reasons why he left his various jobs.

c) Anything about the applicant that is personal, i.e. his character, habits, interests, etc.

Using only the information given, write, in three separate paragraphs of no more than 50 words each, what you will tell your boss.

DIRECTOR: Do sit down, Mr Fisher. Cigarette?

MR FISHER: No thank you, I don't smoke.

DIRECTOR: Well, that's going to make life easier for you if we offer you the job, because we've just started an anti-smoking campaign among the office staff.
Now, looking through your curriculum vitae, I see you were trained first of all as an architect. Why did you change to being a personnel officer?

MR FISHER: My main reason, I suppose, was that there were so few jobs going for architects at the time when I finished my training. I did work for a little while in an architect's office, but mainly as a superior office boy, and I really couldn't see any opportunity for advancement there. I felt my training was being wasted.

DIRECTOR: I see, so you went into personnel work for a rather negative reason then, did you?

MR FISHER: To begin with, I must confess, my idea was to find an alternative to architecture as quickly as possible, and it didn't really matter what that alternative was. I began a personnel officer's course at night school and after about three months at it I became really interested.

DIRECTOR: Can I just interrupt one moment? Were you still working in the architect's office during this time?

MR FISHER: Yes I was, but shortly after that I gave it up because I was accepted to do personnel management at Bloxter Polytechnic.

DIRECTOR: And after your three years there you started work in the Shaw Motor Company.

MR FISHER: That's right. I was there for five years working in a large department, under Mr Ford – I believe you know him.

DIRECTOR: Yes indeed. He was personnel manager here before going to Shaw's. Well, may I ask why you left Shaw's? It's an excellent company to work for.

MR FISHER: If I am honest, the reason I left was that Mr Ford was obviously going to stay there for the rest of his working life, and so there would have been no chance for me to become head of the department; and I'm the kind of person who wants to get on in life.

DIRECTOR: I see. I think the rest of your experience is clear from the curriculum vitae – three years with Driscoll's and you left because they went out of business, and about four years with your present employers. Tell me a little bit about yourself when you're not working, Mr Fisher.

MR FISHER: Well, I'm very keen on games – squash and tennis in particular, and I enjoy watching horse-racing; but I suppose most of my spare time I spend looking after my bees.

DIRECTOR: Bees! That's an unusual hobby. Tell me . . .

Set 3

PAPER 1 Reading Comprehension (1 hour)

Section A

In this section you must choose the word or phrase which best completes each sentence. Give one answer only to each question.

1 I don't know where it is, but I must have ...... it somewhere
   A let   B forgotten   C missed   D left

2 The travel agency provided us with a lot of thick colour ...... to look through.
   A prospects   B brochures   C catalogues   D leaflets

3 ...... of the election, many schools were closed for the day.
   A Because   B For   C Due   D As

4 One way to get rid of hiccups is to ...... your breath for as long as possible.
   A take   B catch   C draw   D hold

5 People have always thought he was poor; in fact he had a good ...... of money hidden under the floor of his house.
   A deal   B much   C part   D many

6 I used to live directly ...... an old lady who kept cats; from my front windows I could see dozens of them moving around in the front room of her cottage.
   A beside   B near   C opposite   D across

7 Which is the best route for me to follow if I want to get to the airport ...... ten o'clock?
   A until   B while   C within   D by

8 'Please get ...... of that white mouse immediately, Gertie!' said Mr Trumper. 'I will not have it in my classroom during lessons.'
   A put   B rid   C away   D out

9 When you retire at the age of sixty or sixty-five, you receive a(n) ...... from the government.
   A pension   B grant   C money   D allowance

10 The ...... of unemployed people has more than doubled in the last five years.
    A figure   B amount   C number   D size

11 I'll see you in the bar in the ...... between Acts I and II.
    A interruption   B pause   C gap   D interval

12 Don't take too much cake, Sarah. Make sure everyone gets a(n) ...... share.
    A own   B fair   C same   D just

13 For goodness' sake, stop .... The whole street will be able to hear you.
    A shouting   B whispering   C smiling   D mumbling

14 I really think the colour is wrong, it doesn't ...... the carpet.
    A fit   B agree   C match   D shade

15 I'm ...... to go to Italy this year.
    A thinking   B hoping   C looking   D awaiting

16 I had to ...... the night in a hotel, the fog was too thick for me to drive any further.
    A rest   B stand   C stay   D remain

17 Hold on ...... to the lifebelt, otherwise you'll sink.
    A strong   B tight   C firm   D steady

18 Do you think you could ...... me your pen until the end of the lesson?
    A borrow   B let   C hire   D lend

19 The ...... audience walked out in disgust.
    A entire   B complete   C main   D full

20 I'm very sorry, I ...... a mistake.
    A do   B make   C made   D did

21 It was a long time before the man ...... stealing the car.
    A admitted   B agreed   C accepted   D argued

22 It's difficult to ...... a driving test at the first attempt.
    A succeed   B reach   C take   D pass

23 The box was a very interesting ......
    A plan   B figure   C shape   D form

24 If you'd like to watch, I'll ...... you how it works.
    A demonstrate   B show   C explain   D say

25 It took her many months to ...... the shock of his death.
    A get round   B get over   C get on with   D get across

Section B

In this section of Reading Comprehension you will find after each of the passages a number of questions or unfinished statements about the passage, each with four suggested answers or ways of finishing. You must choose the one which you think fits best. **Give one answer only** to each question. Read each passage right through before choosing your answers.

First passage

They went up the narrow steps to the level of the stage. The voices of the actors became more distinct. He caught the tail-end of a line he recognised. There already? Recurrent fear gripped his stomach.

He looked out on to the brightly lit stage, at the actors moving about, talking, and across to where the girl who was acting as prompter sat with an open script on her knee.   (5)
'Shirley hasn't had a thing to do so far,' Mrs Bostock murmured. 'The whole thing's gone like a dream.' She took the script from Albert's hands and found the place for him. 'Here you are. Now you just follow the action in there and relax, take it easy. You'll be on and off so quick you'll hardly know you've left the wings.'

'I'm all right now,' Albert told her.   (10)

He realised to his own surprise that he was; and he became increasingly so as the action of the play absorbed him, so that he began to feel himself part of it and no longer a frightened amateur shivering in the wings.

Two pages to go. The younger son was telling his brother about the accident. The row was just beginning and at the very height of it he would make his entrance. He began to   (15)
feel excited. What was it Mrs Bostock had said? 'From the second you step on you dominate the stage. Your entrance is like a thunder-clap.' By shots! He realised vaguely that Mrs Bostock had left his side, but he didn't care now. He felt a supreme confidence. He was ready. He'd show them. By shots he would!

One page. 'You've been rotten all your life, Paul,' the elder brother was saying, 'I've   (20)
never cherished any illusions about you, but this, this is more than even I dreamed you were capable of.'

'I know you hate me, Tom. I've always known it. But if only for father's sake, you must help me now. You know what it will do to him if he finds out. He couldn't stand it in his condition.'   (25)

'You swine. You utter swine...'

The girl who was the maid appeared at his side. She gave him a quick smile. No nerves about her. She'd been on and off the stage all evening, living the part. Albert stared out, fascinated. Not until this moment had he known the true thrill of acting, of submerging one's own personality in that of another. (30)

'Where are you going?'

'I'm going to find that man you knocked down and get him to a hospital. And you're coming with me.'

'But it's too late. Tom. It was hours ago. Someone's sure to have found him by now. Perhaps the police...' (35)

Any minute now. They were working up to his entrance. *Like a thunder-clap*. Albert braced his shoulders and touched his helmet. He glanced down at the script and quickly turned a page. He had lost his place. Panic smote him like a blow. They were still talking, though, so he must be all right. And anyway the maid gave him his cue and she was still by his side. Then suddenly she was no longer at his side. She had gone. He fumbled with (40) his script. Surely... not so far...

He felt Mrs Bostock at his elbow. He turned to her in stupid surprise.

'But,' he said, 'they've... they've...'

She nodded. 'Yes. They've skipped three pages. They've missed your part right out.'

From *The Desperadoes* by Stan Barstow

26 How important was Albert's part in the play?
   A He was the principal actor
   B His part was short but dramatic
   C He had to pretend to be frightened
   D His part was long and difficult

27 What would he 'show them'?
   A How excited he was
   B How well he could act
   C How rotten the younger brother was
   D How much he cared about it all

28 The younger brother in the play
   A had injured someone in an accident
   B hated his brother
   C couldn't understand his father's condition
   D disapproved of what his older brother had done

29 Why did Albert feel a sense of panic?
   A It was about his entrance
   B He heard a thunder-clap
   C They were still talking
   D He thought he had lost his place

30 What had gone wrong?
   A The maid had made a mistake
   B Mrs Bostock had made a mistake
   C The actors on stage had made a mistake
   D Albert had made a mistake

31 In this section of the play who was on the stage that night?
   A Mrs Bostock, the maid and two brothers
   B Shirley and two brothers
   C Albert and two brothers
   D The two brothers

Second passage

Madame Tussaud's Exhibition of Waxworks was originally opened in Paris in 1770 by her uncle, Dr Curtius. Madame Tussaud herself made her earliest surviving portrait, that of Voltaire, when she was 17 and then spent the next few years teaching Louis XVI's young sister the art of modelling in wax. During the French Revolution Madame Tussaud and her uncle moulded the heads of almost every distinguished victim of the guillotine: the death (5) heads of Louis XVI and Marie Antoinette, and also of some of the revolutionaries can still be seen in the Chamber of Horrors in the exhibition's permanent home in London's Marylebone Road, next to Baker Street underground station.

In 1802, as sole owner of the exhibition since her uncle's death, Madame Tussaud left France for England and opened at the Lyceum Theatre in London. For 33 years she set up (10) her exhibition in assembly rooms, hotels, town halls and theatres throughout Britain. Then, at the age of 75 when she was tired of travelling, she settled in London where she continued to make wax models until she was 81 and to sit at her table in the exhibition almost to the year of her death in 1850.

Madame Tussaud was the first of five generations to be involved in the art of wax (15) modelling, and the methods and processes used by the artists in the studios today have changed little since the founding of the exhibition. Whenever possible, the subject is invited to Tussaud's studios or visited by Tussaud's artists so that notes, measurements and photographs can be taken for reference. Because wax is so very fragile, the body and limbs of the figures are made in plaster – only the parts of the body which show, heads and (20) hands, in the majority of cases, are made in wax. Real human hair is used on the head and each strand is cut into the scalp one at a time. Approximately 300 strands of hair per square inch are individually inserted – a task often taking three to four weeks to complete. For a totally convincing facial expression the careful setting of the eyes is essential, and surgical glass eyes of precisely the right size and colour are used. Finally clothes, often (25) donated by the subjects themselves, complete the life-like model.

32 The model of Voltaire
    A was the first model Madame Tussaud ever made
    B was made when he was 17
    C was made by Dr Curtius
    D has not been destroyed

33 Madame Tussaud's exhibition
    A has no permanent home
    B is in Paris
    C is in the Chamber of Horrors
    D has been in London for over 100 years

34 The Tussaud models
    A have been made in a similar way for 200 years
    B take three to four weeks to complete
    C are often donated by the subjects themselves
    D used to be made of wax, but are now made of plaster

35 Madame Tussaud was born in
    A 1750
    B 1760
    C 1770
    D 1780

36 Madame Tussaud's uncle
    A was a victim of the guillotine
    B owned the exhibition but did not make models
    C was always sole owner of the exhibition
    D made some models which can still be seen today

Third passage

What is Swiftair?

Swiftair is an express airmail service to all countries

What are the advantages of Swiftair?
All airmail carrying the Swiftair label receives special and separate handling in the U.K. And priority treatment in those countries of destination which operate an express delivery service. These countries are listed on the back of this leaflet.

How much time does Swiftair save?
The Post Office aims for Swiftair items to be flown to the country of destination the day after posting, subject to the availability of flights. And to be delivered at least one day earlier than regular airmail.

To obtain the best possible service, you should post before the latest recommended posting time to London in your area (or to Glasgow in the case of Scotland).

How much does Swiftair cost?
Regular airmail rates plus the £1.50 Swiftair fee – whatever the destination.

What can be sent by Swiftair in Europe?
Letters, packets, newspapers and periodicals (All-up items on the Post Office Register).

Weight limit: 2 kgs.
Printed papers, which do not qualify for the newspaper and periodical rates, may be sent as All-up letters, if sealed and paid at the higher rate, and do not exceed 2 kgs.

What can be sent by Swiftair outside Europe?
Airmail letters, printed papers and small packets.

Weight limit:
2 kgs for letters and most printed papers. 5 kgs for books and pamphlets. 1 kg for small packets.

How do I use Swiftair?
You can get individual Swiftair labels, or sheets of labels, at any post office. Just affix your Swiftair express delivery label to the top left hand corner of the address side. In the case of items going outside Europe, affix it immediately below the airmail label. Add the normal postage plus the Swiftair fee.

Items should then be handed over a post office counter, or included in your firm's collections – but separated from other items to ensure proper handling. And to make life easier, you can pay using either stamps or meter franks.

Swiftair Extras
You can register or insure your Swiftair items to most countries on payment of the appropriate additional fee. (For all these fees, see the Postal Rates Overseas Leaflet or Compendium). A certificate of posting will be supplied free of charge on request at the time of posting.

What about customs declarations for merchandise?
Swiftair items containing merchandise must bear the small, green Douane C1 label. If the value of the merchandise exceeds £270.00, then the C2/CP3 form must be used.

NB. Express Delivery Service
This is still available for AIR AND SURFACE PARCELS, PRINTED PAPERS TO EUROPE and SURFACE LETTERS AND PRINTED PAPERS TO COUNTRIES OUTSIDE EUROPE. The rate is given in the Postal Rates Overseas Leaflets and the Compendium.

37 Swiftair letters, etc. are delivered
    A more quickly in certain countries
    B 24 hours earlier in all countries
    C the day after posting
    D more quickly in all countries

38 When sending letters by Swiftair
    A you must go to a post office
    B you can use a post box
    C you must not mix Swiftair with ordinary letters
    D you must address letters on the top left hand corner

39 What advantage does Swiftair have over ordinary mail?
    A It is safer
    B It is always quicker
    C Delays are less likely
    D It is cheaper

40 What kind of items can be sent by Swiftair outside Europe?
    A Letters, packets up to 2 kg, newspapers and periodicals
    B Any item up to 5 kg
    C Air and surface parcels
    D Airmail letters up to 2 kg, and a few other items

PAPER 2 Composition (1½ hours)

Write **two only** of the following composition exercises. Your answers must follow exactly the instructions given, and must be of between 120 and 180 words each.

1 A friend is coming to visit you in your town for the first time. Unfortunately, you have an important interview, and will not be able to meet him/her at the station; so you have asked your sister/brother to go in your place. Write a letter to your friend explaining the situation and describing your sister/brother so your friend will recognise him or her at the station. You should make the beginning and ending like those of an ordinary letter, but the address is not to be counted in the number of words.

2 What, in your opinion, is the most important invention or discovery of this century? Give reasons for your opinion.

3 Write an article for your college magazine about the lack of things to do for young people in your town.

4 Continue the story, 'I was only five years old at the time, but I remember it well...'

5 Base your answer to the following question on your reading of *any* book which you have read recently, or know well.*

Say in what way the place or places in which the story takes place are important.

PAPER 3 Use of English (2 hours)

1 Fill in each of the numbered blanks in the passage with one suitable word.

One of the problems I have when I (1) ...... my dentist is that he always insists (2) ...... carrying on conversations with me although it is quite impossible (3) ...... me to (4) ...... a single word in reply.

    The last time I went to see him was when I had already (5) ...... rather severe toothache for two or three days, and I was in considerable (6) .... (7) ...... told me that a tooth (8) ...... have to be taken out, the dentist gave me an injection and filled my mouth (9) ...... various pads and instruments (10) ...... made speech (11) ...... out of the question. He then began work on my tooth, chattering on as he worked about (12) ...... subject under the sun: his children, his dogs, his car, the holiday he and his family had just had, and so on. I (13) ...... several attempts to communicate with him, but the (14) ...... things that came out of my mouth were meaningless noises and, eventually, my tooth.

    The dentist went on talking and I went on trying to say (15) ...... I wanted to (16) ...... him, but of course (17) ...... the time I was able to speak again it was too late! I confirmed with my tongue what I had (18) ...... from the start, and what I had desperately (19) ...... trying to say to the dentist: he had taken out (20) ...... wrong tooth!

2 Finish each of the following sentences in such a way that it means exactly the same as the sentence printed before it.

Example:
It took me an hour to get here today.
I spent ....
Answer: I spent an hour getting here today.

*The prescribed books on which this type of question is based will vary from year to year.

a) The only thing I have forgotten to do is cancel the milk.
I've remembered .. *to do everything but cancel the milk*

b) He's too short to get a job as a policeman.
He isn't .. *tall enough to get a job as a policeman*

c) He paid very little for his motor-bike.
His motor-bike didn't .. *cost him a lot*

d) Nobody does it better than you.
There isn't .. *anybody who does it better than you*

e) It is said that English people are quiet and reserved.
English people are .. *said to be quiet and reserved*

f) It is very rare for the police to stop cars without a good reason.
Cars .. *are rarely stopped by the police without a good*

g) 'I wouldn't sail too close to the rocks, if I were you,' she said to Roger.
She advised .. *Roger not to sail too close to the rocks*

h) You really should do something about that broken stone on the path.
It's time you .. *did sth*

i) She is still working on her book.
She hasn't .. *finished working on her book*

j) I don't live in a big city so unfortunately I can't go to the cinema very often.
If I .. *as often as I like*

3 Write in the space in each of the following sentences the correct phrase made from **put**.

Example:
'I'm ...... to Mr Jones now,' said the telephonist.
Answer: putting you through

a) Because of injuries to several players, the match was *put off* until the following week.
b) *Put away* your toys, please. I don't want them all over the floor.
c) It's very difficult to *put up with* other people's bad habits.
d) Please don't keep interrupting when I'm counting the stock, you're *putting me off*
e) You won't have anywhere to stay when you get to London, but Jane will be happy to *put you up*

4 Write in the space in each of the following sentences the correct word to describe the piece of paper.

Example:
'Excuse me, waiter. Could we have our ...... please?'
Answer: bill

a) 'Take this *prescription* to the chemist and he'll make it up for you,' said the doctor.
b) I've got a very good *receipt* for chicken soup. Do you want to borrow it?
c) You can't stay on a bus unless you've got a *ticket*
d) Shops will only exchange faulty goods if the customer is able to show the *receipt*
e) If you give me your *list* of things you want, I'll do your shopping for you.

5 Make all the changes and additions necessary to produce, from the following seven sets of words and phrases, seven sentences which together make a complete letter from Ahmet to his friend Gökhan back home in Istanbul. Note carefully from the example what kind of alterations need to be made.

Example:
I/wonder/why you/not/reply/last letter.

Answer: I was wondering why you had not replied to my last letter.

Dear Gökhan,

a) Well, as you/see/post-card/here I/be/Oxford. In fact/I/be/here/two weeks now.
b) I/stay/old Turkish friend/who/study/university here.
c) I/think/you/be/interested/know/the first thing/I/do/when I arrive/England/be/find/Turkish restaurant.
d) I/go/see/all/famous buildings/London/last week.
e) Next week I/go/Scotland/and if I/have/time/I hope/be able/go/Wales.
f) How/be/your family? You/start/new job/yet?
g) I/be/sorry/you/can not/come/with me/this trip/but perhaps we/manage/another trip/before we/be/too old!
        Yours,
           Ahmet

6 Study the map below and answer the questions which follow.

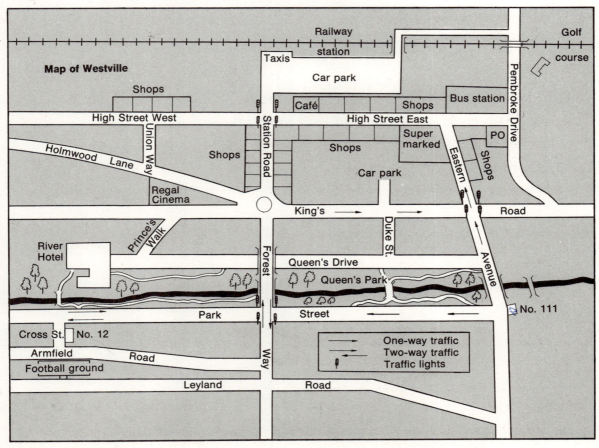

a) You are standing outside the railway station and a stranger asks you where the post office is. Tell him how to get there. ('PO' is the post office).

b) Explain to a friend who is staying at No. 111 Eastern Avenue how to get to the Regal Cinema on foot.

c) You are standing in the High Street outside the bus station and you want to get to your friend's house at No. 12 Cross Street. Someone gives you directions: write what he said.

d) You are sitting in a café on the High Street and are asked by a group of young people (all wearing red and white scarves) how to find the football stadium. Tell them politely!